Have you heard the
GOOD NEWS?

The Simplicity of Sharing the Gospel Effectively

NICK KINN

MW00744792

Dedication

I would like to dedicate this book to my wife Jane, for her continual support of the ministry that God has called me to do. To encourage me to press into the higher calling of God in Christ Jesus. I would also like to thank my parents, Alex and Ruby Kinn for bringing me into this world. And I would like to give a special thanks to my pastors Mac and Lynne Hammond, who are my spiritual parents, equipping me with the word of God for the past 21 years, so I can do the work of the evangelist!

Have You Heard the Good News:
The Simplicity of Sharing the Gospel Effectively

ISBN 0-9753294-0-5
All rights reserved.
Unless otherwise indicated, all Scripture quotations
are from the King James Version.
Copyright ©2004

Content

Preface

I wrote this book because I'm lit with a flame that cannot be quenched. It is a flame that never recedes. It compels me, propels me, and drives me. It is the fire of soul winning.

The end is near, this we all know. This awareness never escapes my thinking. It feeds a growing urgency – there is little time to harvest the fields. And the harvest fields are white, ready for harvest. Where are the laborers?

Brothers and sisters, that is the cry of my heart. Where are the laborers? Lost souls unaware they're on their way to hell… souls without hope, who have given up… souls deceived, vexed, in anguish… all waiting for someone to shine the light of Jesus on their lives.

The time is short. God is sounding the trumpet to round up His army, to send them forth into the fields. All Christians are called. All Christians are needed.

God used a book to ignite in me His vision for the world, to ignite in me His urgency, to ignite in me His great love for the lost. My prayer is that He will use this book to do that same work in you.

May you be lit with a flame that cannot be quenched – a flame that never recedes. That compels you, propels you, and drives you – the fire of soul winning.

Forward

I have known Nick Kinn since he first started coming to my church in 1982. It wasn't long before I noticed he had an extraordinary anointing on him for one-on-one evangelism. On his own volition, Nick spent many hours every week on the streets of downtown Minneapolis sharing Jesus with everyone he met. He soon infused other believers with his zeal for lost souls and convinced them to join him on the streets.

Over the years, Nick was faithful and steadfast in street evangelism. His zeal never waned. It was obvious that this was his calling, and in 1986, I asked Nick to join my staff as head of the evangelism ministry. Since then he has trained and led hundreds of believers in street evangelism, with the result being tremendous fruit for the kingdom of God. He and his ministry teams literally go into the highways and byways of our city, winning souls for the Lord. They go into prisons, nursing homes, and reservations bringing hope to a hopeless people. They go to cities across our nation and "blitz" it with the Gospel. And they go to the uttermost parts of the earth, preaching Jesus to the nations. Through these different avenues, over 500,000 souls have come to a saving knowledge of our Lord and Savior Jesus Christ!

Good news travels fast. Churches began to hear of our success with winning souls. Nick began to receive invitations from other churches to teach and train them in one-on-one evangelism. The results were the same. Every church came alive with the fire of soul winning. Churches that could only account for a few souls being won to the Lord were now giddy with excitement after praying with hundreds and some thousands to receive Jesus!

It is my pleasure to introduce you to the ministry of Nick Kinn. As you read this book, may you too experience the fire of evangelism!

James M. Hammond

Chapter One

How I Came to Know the Lord

The first time I came in contact with a born again Christian was when I was 18 years old. One of my coworkers, Lyle, loved God and never passed up an opportunity to share his faith. Consequently, all the other guys used to persecute and mock him endlessly.

One day I thought I would score a few points with my friends and said, "I'm going to pull this guy's leg and pretend I'm saved." Feigning Christian zeal, I walked up to him and said, "Hey, Lyle, Jesus is coming soon! Isn't that right? He's coming back." All the guys stood off to the side watching, laughing their heads off the whole time.

Lyle knew I was making fun of him, but he walked in love toward me and responded by saying, "Yes, the Lord is coming soon," and then proceeded to tell me about the rapture and end-time events.

I didn't know it at the time, but that exposure to Lyle in 1969 was the beginning of God working in my heart. After I gave my life to the Lord, I remembered back to the Christians that God had set in my path and who planted His incorruptible seed in my heart. I'll always be grateful for their boldness and Christ-like example.

My next contact with a Christian was in 1970. I was drafted into the army and was sent to Ft. Knox, Kentucky for basic training. One day I was in the laundry room and this woman started telling me about the Lord, saying you had to be born again. She was nice and I didn't want to be rude, so I just hemmed and hawed with her.

When basic training was over, I was shipped out to Ft. Ord, California. At that time, I began to drink a lot. This one particular day, I drank so much that I passed out on my bed. Suddenly I was jolted out of my drunken stupor by the sound of MPs pounding loudly on the windows and yelling at us to get out because someone threatened to blow up the barracks. To my surprise, when I came to I was instantly sober.

After the bomb scare was over, we went into the kitchen. One of the cooks asked me this pointed question: "If you had died tonight, would you have gone to Heaven?" I had to honestly say, "I really don't know if I would." He then began to share with me his testimony, how Jesus delivered him from alcoholism. Again, I just brushed him off like I did the others and said, "Hey, I'm really happy for you, but I'm okay."

And yet another time in the military, there was a Christian who worked in the supply department who handed out weapons to us. One day he handed me an M16 rifle and asked me, "Soldier, if you died today, would you go to heaven?" I said, "Boy, I sure hope so." He told me, "You can know for sure." He then proceeded to tell me his testimony of how God set him free from being a junkie hooked on LSD. In my mind, I tried to justify myself with the fact that I was only an alcoholic and had never done hard drugs. As he shared his testimony of how bad he was, I thought to myself, *If you're going to heaven, then so am I.*

The next seed God planted in my heart was in 1972. I was out of the military and now living on my own. One day I had intentions of going out with a woman who bartended at a local bar. Before I left the apartment, I noticed a piece of paper someone slipped under my door. I picked it up and discovered it was a Christian tract. I read it all the way through. It was so anointed that I wept. In hindsight, I believe someone prayed over it. I got convicted and, as a result, decided against going out with the bartender.

In 1974, my sister Susan got saved and like most Christians her family became her mission field. She intended to get every one of us saved. She arranged for this Baptist Pastor to come over and talk about being born again to my brother-in-law and me. Using a Chic tract, he explained to us how to get saved. We didn't take him seriously for a second and laughed behind his back the entire time. When he was done, he asked us, "Are you ready to make a decision to make Jesus your Lord?" We wanted to get out of there so we could finish drinking our ripple wine so I quoted the only scripture I knew and said, "Doesn't the Bible say that when a man prays he should go into his closet and shut the door? I think I'll just wait and go into my closet to pray." My brother-in-law chimed in with me. When he left, we laughed our heads off.

Two years later on Easter Sunday in 1976, I had another encounter with a Christian coworker and this time I wasn't laughing. The fact that I had to work on Easter Sunday made me mad. I was in the break room letting off steam about it. My coworker, Mike, walked up to me and asked me point blank, "What does Easter mean to you?" I retorted, "A ham dinner and time with my family."

Like all the other Christians before him, he began to share with me his testimony. He said, "You know, Nick, one time someone once asked me the question, 'If you died, would you go to heaven?' And at the time, I really didn't know. But I know today." He shared with me the events of his life that led up to him getting saved. He said he was married to a born again Christian and cheated on her. One day he decided to leave her and move to another state. But before he left, he was going to do a "job" on her. He punched her so hard in the face he knocked out a tooth. He walked out the door and never looked back.

Months later he was partying with a group of people and had an experience that caused him to rethink the direction his life was going. The party was outside and he accidentally fell down a cliff that had a 100-foot drop. Miraculously, he came out of it completely unharmed, not even a scratch. Mike told me, "Right there, I got on my knees and prayed, 'Jesus, if You're real, come into my heart and change me.' I went home to the same woman I had punched in the face and told her that I had accepted Jesus. She forgave me for everything I had done to her and took me back."

I was not only interested in what he was saying, but I was truly touched by his story. This was the only Christian I didn't make fun of. Mike gave me a book to read by Salem Kirban called, 666. I took the book and read it that weekend. God began to work on my heart because of that book. I was an alcoholic and I knew it. I remember being at my sister Julie's wedding in June 1976. With a beer in my hand, I walked up to my uncle who is a Pentecostal preacher and said, "Uncle Art, would you pray for me?"

Two months later on my birthday, August 21, 1976, I went to a Minnesota Kicks soccer game with a couple of friends. After the game, we went to a local bar and I told them about the book that Mike gave me.

The book is about a guy who was married to a Christian. One day she just disappeared, having gone up in the rapture. It made you think. In fact, I had been thinking about it a lot. While in the bar, I shared with my friends about this book, and I was so engrossed in the conversation that I didn't even take one drink of beer. Remembering back, I wasn't a Christian but it was as though there was an anointing on me as I spoke. They were a captive audience, glued to my every word.

That night after I got home, I got on my knees at three in the morning and I prayed, "Jesus, if You're real, come into my heart. I'm tired of being a drunk." He came! His presence was so strong that I was almost slain in the Spirit. The peace of God flooded my heart. I got so excited that I couldn't wait to tell everyone about what had happened.

The next day at work I told the Christians I got saved and they were real excited for me. But I got a different reaction from all my drinking buddies. Right away, they started mocking me. "You're born again, huh? Are you wearing diapers now? Can you drive a car?" It really hurt. I was crushed by their reaction. But the Lord ministered to me immediately. I had brought my Bible with me to work. I opened it and it fell on Matthew 5:11-12. My eyes fell on the verse, "Blessed are you when men persecute you and say all manner of evil against you falsely for My name's sake, for great is your reward in heaven, for so persecuted they the prophets which were before you." After that, the hurt went away and I had peace again. I had only been saved two days when God gave me that scripture.

I had good fellowship with the other Christians at work. We had Bible studies and prayed on our breaks. Three years later, I got filled with the Spirit and I started attending a particular ministry and started going door-to-door witnessing. I got real disenchanted with it. People slammed doors in my face. No one got saved. I wanted so much to lead someone to the Lord. One night in April 1979, I got on my knees and prayed, "Jesus, I've been saved three years and I've never prayed with anybody to receive You." In response, the Lord quickened to my heart the scripture, "Delight thyself in the Lord and He will give you the desires of your heart." (Ps. 37:4)

At the time I was in the Amway business. That night I had an Amway meeting and after the meeting, I gave an altar call and a lady got saved. I was so excited. I thought it was appropriate for her to get saved at an Amway meeting, because it's a cleaning business and she just cleaned up her life. Glory to God!

Soon after that, my sister Patty invited me to visit her church, Living Word Christian Center. I did and in January 1982, I made Living Word my home church. Later, I met my wife Jane there and we were married in August 1985.

Shortly after this, I read a book by Marie Chapian entitled, *Escape From Rage*. It was the testimony of a man who was a pastor of a local Twin Cities' church. He was a drug addict and lived on the streets of Minneapolis. His lifestyle was as low as you could go. God saved him and brought him out of the gutter, and Roger was instrumental in bringing thousands of people to God. That book had a powerful impact on me. God deposited an intense compassion for the lost and a passion to tell them about Jesus. After reading that book, I remember walking down Hennepin Avenue, a sin-infested section of our city, weeping for lost souls. I started walking that avenue every week, telling everyone I met about Jesus.

Then I'll never forget the day, April 10, 1982, when my pastor prophesied over me. He said, "Not hundreds, but thousands will be won to the Lord through you and that every person who becomes your friend will be in heaven because of the boldness to win souls that is on you." At that time, I was still going out on the streets to witness alone. Once in a while, one or two people would pray with me to receive Jesus. There was little fruit.

Then I hooked up with a guy from my church, Peter, and he and I went out together as a team. Shortly after that things started to escalate. We started to see four or five people get saved every time we went out.

One night in 1984, Peter and I were walking down Hennepin Avenue and out of his spirit he said, "One of these days there will be so many laborers coming out with you that you'll need school buses to drive them all down here." That came to pass when we started having all-church evangelism outings. One time, we had as many as 400 people go out.

In 1986, I was thrilled when my pastor put me in charge of the evangelism ministry at church and then in May 1988, I came on staff full-time as the evangelism pastor. The ministry kept increasing. News of the success of our evangelism outreach started to spread and churches from other states began to ask me to come to their church to teach them how to evangelize their communities.

Soon God started sending us on missions trips to other parts of the world. One of the first times I went to Peru, I did an evangelism seminar way out in the boon docks with our missionary from Living Word. He spoke on the baptism of the Holy Spirit, and I spoke on evangelism. The service went five hours and 79 people prayed to receive Jesus and 179 were filled with the

Spirit. We started praying for people to get healed and I witnessed many miraculous healings. One lady testified that before she came to our meeting she couldn't hear or speak. This was the first miracle that I had ever experienced! The deaf hear, the dumb speak. Another man said, he had a tumor on his stomach and it immediately dissolved. I wept. I had never before witnessed the things that were happening that day. Since then, God has opened up many wonderful opportunities for me to share Jesus. I give Him all the glory.

The most fulfilling experience any Christian can have is to lead another person into the saving knowledge of the Lord Jesus Christ. No other experience comes close to it. As I've been faithful to share the good news of the Gospel, God has fulfilled the all-consuming desire of my heart – leading countless numbers of people to Jesus. My desire for you is to experience that same joy in leading others to the Lord.

Chapter Two

The Five A's
of Evangelism

Most Christians I know have a strong desire to serve God. They long to be used by God in some way. They spend great amounts of time in prayer, seeking His plan for their life. They busy themselves with all kinds of activity, attending prayer groups and Bible studies. They listen to tapes and read books. They're in church every time the doors are open. Yet they're still frustrated because God isn't using them in ministry the way they'd like to be used.

I'm always perplexed by this behavior. I wonder why they pray for direction when all they need to do is read their Bible to know God's will for them. Don't get me wrong. I'm not trying to say that seeking God for His will or being active in church is wrong. That's not the point I'm trying to make. I simply wonder why there aren't more believers obeying what I call, the "11th commandment!"

What is the 11th commandment? It was the command Jesus gave to all believers, right before He ascended into heaven.

Go ye into all the world, and preach the Gospel to every creature. He that believeth and is baptized shall be saved; but he that believeth not shall be damned, Mark 16:15-16.

Many Christians have the mistaken idea this commandment was meant only for those who stand in the five-fold office of the evangelist. On the contrary, this command to go into all the world and preach the Gospel was directed to every believer.

Christians long to see the power of God in their lives. But there seems to be a power shortage in most Christians. Yet, the Bible says signs and wonders should be following us. Look at the next verse.

And these signs shall follow them that believe; in my name they shall cast out devils; they shall speak with new tongues; they shall take up serpents; and if they drink any deadly thing, it shall not hurt them; they shall lay hands on the sick and they shall recover. (Mark 16:15-18)

These signs will follow them that "believe." Are you a believer? Then these signs should be following you. I think most, if not all, believers would like this scripture to be a reality in their lives, but sadly this is not the case. Why isn't it? The reason, I believe, can be found in verse twenty.

And they went forth, and preached every where, the Lord working through them and confirming the word with signs following. (Mark 16:20)

Do you see it? Jesus said to His disciples, "Go." They obeyed the command and "they went." What was the result of their obedience? God confirmed His Word with signs and wonders "following." This is where most Christians are missing it. They fail to obey Jesus' command to "go." Do you want signs and wonders to follow you? Then you must first obey the command of Jesus to "go."

Many of you hunger, even ache, to do wonderful things for God in Jesus' name. How can God do signs and wonders through you if you do not go and preach His Word? Brothers and sisters, I don't say these things to condemn or offend you. It's just that I've seen so many believers waiting for God to set them in ministry positions, but they haven't even been faithful to share Jesus to their coworker, their neighbor, or even their families. Like I said, Christians spend far too much time seeking God in prayer, wondering if they're called to the ministry. If that's you, stop praying. You are. In fact, every Christian is called of God to be a minister. Look at 2 Corinthians 5:17-18:

Therefore if any man be in Christ, he is a new creature: old things are passed away; behold, all things are become new. And all things are of God, who hath reconciled us to himself by Jesus Christ, and hath given to us the ministry of reconciliation.

You are a minister of reconciliation. You say, "Brother Nick, I'm not qualified to be a minister." Yes, you are. If you are born again, you are a minister of reconciliation. That's the only qualification you need. You don't have to have a P.H.D. You don't have to have a framed license hanging on your wall. You don't have to have a bunch of initials behind your name. You are a minister of reconciliation.

What is a minister of reconciliation?

Simply put, I'm talking about evangelism. Every Christian is called to participate in evangelism. That's what a minister of reconciliation is.

The Five "A's" of Evangelism

I'd like to share with you the five "A's" of evangelism – Assignment, Ability, Authority, Anointing and, lastly, Availability. I'm going to give you a lot of scriptures, most of which should be very familiar to you. Please don't skim past them; instead, I want you to read them word for word. In fact, say them out loud to yourself so you can get them down into your heart. When I'm done, you'll know beyond a doubt what God's will is for you regarding *your* part in fulfilling the Great Commission.

God Gave You an Assignment

Let's begin with the first "A" of evangelism – Assignment. Jesus has "assigned" us with an assignment. The definition of the word *assign* means 1. To set apart for a particular purpose, 2. To select for a duty or office; appoint 3. To give out as a task; allot. The word *assignment* means 1. Something, such as a task, that is assigned, 2. A position or post of duty to which one is assigned.

Jesus assigned us with the assignment to go to all nations, to baptize them, and teach them about Jesus. In fact, Jesus chose you for this duty. John 15:16. "Ye have not chosen me, but I have chosen you and ordained you that ye should go and bring forth fruit, and that your fruit should remain."

Isn't that great! God chose you and ordained you to bear fruit – to get souls saved for the kingdom of God.

Now I want you to look at this scripture in John 17. While Jesus was praying to the Father, He said, "As thou hast sent Me into the world, even so have I sent them into the world." Jesus thinks so highly of you and me that He has sent us into the world just as God sent Him into the world.

In Ephesians 5:16, we are told to redeem the time because the days are evil. The darkness that is in the world is getting darker. All you have to do is turn on the news to find that out. The news media daily report on nations who are at war with one another. We hear of Hitler-esque atrocities being committed against whole societies of people in the name of war – acts of brutality and inhumanity at mass levels. Cataclysmic events are on the increase – earthquakes, floods, tornadoes, volcanic eruptions – all resulting in great loss of human life and economic devastation.

It's hard for people to find anything positive to say about the world in which we live today. People are frightened to leave their home. They're even more terrified for their children's future. Will they even have a future? They feel hopeless. They need someone to show them the Way. How can we sit back on our laurels and not share with them the hope of salvation? How can we deny them from hearing the Gospel? You say, "I'm not denying anyone from hearing the Gospel." Dear friend, if you never open your mouth and tell them about Jesus, your silence is the same as denying them the Good News.

Freely you have received. Will you freely give?

God Gave You His Ability

Now let's talk about the second "A" of evangelism – Ability. God has given us His ability to accomplish His assignment. I have had the wonderful privilege of traveling all over the world to speak in churches, encouraging them to fulfill God's assignment. I have heard of every reason why someone couldn't go out on the streets to share Jesus. Yet, I know people really do want to lead others to Christ. Their apprehension stems from thinking they have no ability.

But did you know that God never expected you to use your own ability to preach the Gospel? It's true. It's the Holy Spirit who anoints us with God's ability. I'll prove it to you in the Word. Look what it says in 2 Corinthians 3:5-6:

Not that we are sufficient of ourselves to think any thing as of ourselves: but our sufficiency is of God; who hath made us able ministers of the New Testament...

It doesn't get any plainer than that. God Himself has made you an able minister of the New Testament. All you have to do is believe it and then act like you believe it. (Look... if I can do it, then so can you.) Now look at Acts 1:8:

> *But ye shall receive power after that the Holy Ghost is come upon you: and ye shall be witnesses unto me both in Jerusalem, and in all Judea, and in Samaria, and unto the uttermost part of the earth.*

My friend, God gave us power to be witnesses for Him. If that's not enough to make you shout, look at Jesus' own words in John 14:12:

> *Verily, verily, I say unto you, he that believeth on Me, the works that I do shall he do also; and greater works than these shall he do; because I go unto My Father.*

It's clear in the Word that Jesus gave us His ability and power to be witnesses for Him. God never meant for us to go forth in our own ability. After I show people in the Word that God has given them all ability to be His witnesses, invariably someone will say to me, "But, Pastor Nick, even though I have the power to be a witness for Jesus, I still don't know *how* to approach someone or *what* to say."

God gives us a practical example of one-on-one evangelism in Acts 8:26-35. You'll see it's a very simple formula. The Lord told Philip to "arise and go." Philip immediately obeyed God and "arose and went." When he saw an Ethiopian eunuch riding in his chariot, the Lord told Philip to go talk to him. The Bible says Philip ran up to the eunuch and "opened his mouth" and told him about Jesus.

There you have it – basic one-on-one evangelism. Arise and go… find someone… approach them… open your mouth… and tell them about Jesus. It really is that simple.

Then there is the excuse I hear so often from people who hate the idea of walking up to a complete stranger and engaging them in conversation. People have such qualms about this, like they're violating some social rule of etiquette. But if you think about it, our society approaches strangers all the time for all kinds of reasons. How many times has this happened to you? You walk into a department store and someone you've never met walks up to you and asks if you'd like to sample their new cologne – and then squirts some of it on you. Haven't we all been approached in a shopping mall by a complete stranger asking us to take a survey? How about telemarketers? People you don't even know call you at your home and asks you all sorts of questions. (Usually right when you're ready to eat supper.) Are you personally acquainted with every door-to-door salesman that's knocked on your door?

Are you getting my point? There's nothing wrong or improper about walking up to a total stranger and talking to them about Jesus. To be honest with you, it wasn't easy for me the first few times I approached a total stranger and tried to witness to them. I felt insecure because I didn't think I knew enough Bible and I was afraid of being rejected.

And we were rejected. In fact, it was down right discouraging. In the beginning, no one would talk to us. They'd snarl, "Get out of my face," Or they'd snap, "I don't want to hear any of that garbage." They'd turn their back on us and walk away. A lady even threw her cigarette at me. No one would take the time to listen to us. At the end of the night when I got in my car to go home, I hurt so bad inside that I wept. Not because of rejection. But because they were lost and didn't know it. Because I knew the Way and they didn't want to hear it.

Truthfully, at times, it was difficult to keep going. But we kept going because of the scripture in 1 Cor. 15:57-58:

> *But thanks be to God, which giveth us the victory through our Lord Jesus Christ. Therefore, my beloved brethren, be ye stedfast, unmoveable, always abounding in the work of the Lord, forasmuch as ye know that your labour is not in vain in the Lord.*

I stood on this scripture in faith. If we were steadfast, immovable and kept doing the work of the Lord, we would reap a harvest. God said our labor would not be in vain. When the going got rough, we encouraged ourselves with this scripture.

But there was another reason I didn't give up. I always reminded myself of my own testimony. As you just read in the previous chapter, God used several Christians to witness to me about Jesus before I prayed to receive Him into my life. I wasn't open to it the first few times either. In fact, I was mean. I mocked them. Or I would simply dismiss them saying it was fine for them, but it wasn't for me. But each one of them deposited in me God's incorruptible Word. The first person who shared Jesus with me planted the seed. Then others came along and watered the seed. That seed began to grow. Finally, a Christian came along and was able to reap the harvest. Praise

God! You see, it doesn't matter if people reject you over and over, because you're still being used of God to deposit His incorruptible seed in them. The Bible says our labor is not in vain.

The day finally came when my witnessing partner, Pete, and I experienced a landslide. In one night, we prayed with a total of five people to accept the Lord. You can't imagine how excited we were. I think we floated home.

In the beginning, we weren't as bold or confident as we are now. We didn't have a lot of wisdom. But we kept lifting up the scripture in James 1:5 where it says if you lack wisdom, to ask God. We asked God for wisdom every time we went out. We asked God in faith believing that when we walked up to someone that He would direct our communication. He was faithful. The more we went out, the more wisdom we gained. This resulted in winning souls to the Lord. Praise God! In Proverbs 11:30 it says:

> *The fruit of the rightous is a tree of life; and He that winneth souls is wise.*

God Gave You Authority

Along with ability, God gave His Church authority. This brings us to the third "A" of evangelism – Authority.

It says in Luke 9:1 that when Jesus sent His 12 disciples out to preach the Gospel, He gave them power and authority over all devils and to heal the sick. And again in Luke 10:19, Jesus sent out seventy more of His disciples into the world and He commissioned them saying, "Behold, I give unto you power to tread on serpents and scorpions, and over all the power of the enemy: and nothing shall by any means hurt you."

We take our teams into the most heavily populated areas of the city. Sometimes that means going into places some would refer to as *seedy*. A variety of people congregate in these areas. Our teams regularly pray with gang members, ex-cons, drug dealers, and so on. Frankly, there's some scary people out there, really on the edge. Sometimes our teams see and hear strange things, even bizarre.

A guy in my ministry, Virgil, experienced one of those bizarre encounters. He approached a man who was walking past him and said, "I am sharing the good news of Jesus…" The man barked, "Get out of here with that. I am the Devil." Virgil walked on and a few seconds later, he heard some commotion behind him. He looked back and saw two police cars, one of which drove right up on the sidewalk to intercept this man. The policemen bolted out of their cars, threw down the "Devil," bound him, and tossed him in the car. A man nearby said to Virgil, "What a testimony. The Devil is bound and on his way to jail." With a sly grin, Virgil told me the next week they prayed with a total of 19 people to receive Jesus in the exact spot where the Devil was bound. Of course, he was just teasing. The point I'm trying to make is that you'll be exposed to an atmosphere that is not exactly wholesome. You'll witness things you don't normally see and hear on a regular basis.

Shirley, another member from my team shared with me an interesting experience. She spotted a pickup truck with literally dozens of young men gathered around it. Feeling prompted by the Spirit, she made a beeline straight for the truck. "Bodies scattered in every direction like fleas jumping off a dog's back," said Shirley. "All of them took off except for three young men in the cab of the truck, who couldn't get out. Their eyes were as big as saucers. I said to them, 'Have I got good news for you.'" She proceeded to share Jesus with them, and all three prayed with her.

Afterward, a street-savvy young man said to her, "Did you know that is a drug truck?" Astonished, Shirley replied, "I didn't have a clue." They immediately stopped in their tracks and gave God thanks for His protection.

One night I was out ministering in a park in Minneapolis and a drunken man staggered up to me and threatened me. I recognized him. The week before he overheard me witnessing to someone on the street. He knew the reason I was in the park was to share Jesus. I looked at him. The expression on his face was pure hatred. He raised his whiskey bottle in the air and was coming toward me. Instantly the scripture in Isaiah 54:17 came to me:

> *No weapon that is formed against thee shall prosper; and every tongue that shall rise up against thee in judgment thou shalt condemn. This is the heritage of the servants of the Lord, and their righteousness is of Me, saith the Lord.*

I turned toward him, looked directly in his face and spoke with authority, "I bind you Devil in the name of Jesus. No weapon formed against me will

22

prosper and every tongue that shall come against me in judgment I condemn." Instantly, he stopped in his tracks. The look of hate disappeared and was replaced by a look of bewilderment. He put the bottle down on the ground, turned, and walked away. I called out to him that Jesus loved him and wanted to save him. But he didn't acknowledge me and just kept walking. Praise God, we have authority in Jesus' name!

Paula, a girl from my ministry, came out with us during Monday night evangelism. She's thankful for the authority Jesus gave to us. A man high on drugs approached her. In his stupor, he mistook her to be a drug dealer. He handed her a 20-dollar bill and asked for some drugs. Paula replied, "I don't have any drugs but I do have some good news..." and proceeded to tell him about Jesus.

He became very angry. So angry that he pulled back his fist to strike her. Paula started to say, "No weapon formed against me shall prosper..." when he threw a punch right at her face. But instead of hitting Paula, his fist hit an invisible wall. Much to his astonishment, his hand was stuck in midair. He couldn't free it. He even used his left hand to try and pry it loose. It wouldn't move. He freaked out and took off running down the street. Isn't God good!

I'll share with you one more incident. One night, I walked up to a man who was casually dressed, out to have a good time but already high on something. I approached and asked, "Would you like to hear some good news?" He turned ugly immediately, snarling at me, "I'm going to kill you." My reaction was to lift my hands toward heaven and say, "Praise God, go ahead. I know where I'm going." I didn't expect what happened next. He dropped to his knees right at my feet and started sobbing. I told him that Jesus loved him and wanted him to join Him in heaven one day. When I asked him if he would like to pray and receive Jesus, he did. We talked for a while and then I gave him a ride home. Isn't God amazing? You never know how God will display His power and authority.

At first, I wasn't going to share these incidents with you, because I thought it might put fear in you about going out on the streets to witness. But then I realized, you might as well know about it. Being forewarned is part of the preparation for these encounters. It's one of the Devil's tactics to try to stop you. It happens only rarely and no one ever gets hurt. God always protects us. Knowing that should encourage you, rather than discourage you.

Right? After all, greater is He that is in you, than he that is in the world. (I John 4:4)

I should interject something here about these kinds of encounters. When someone speaks ugly or hatefully to you, you have to remind yourself they are not your enemy. It's Satan who is using them as a tool of harassment against you. Our battle isn't with them. Our battle is with Satan. Ephesians 6:12 says, "For we do not wrestle against flesh and blood, but against principalities, against powers, against the rulers of the darkness of this age, against spiritual hosts of wickedness in the heavenly places." Don't argue with them or threaten them back. Take authority over the Devil to get the situation under control, and then get out of their presence.

God Has Anointed You

This brings us to the fourth "A" of evangelism – Anointing. In Luke 4, we read about when Jesus was anointed by God to begin His earthly ministry. After Jesus was baptized by John the Baptist in the river Jordan, the Holy Spirit led Him into the wilderness for 40 days and while there was tempted by Satan. After Jesus resisted all of Satan's temptations, Jesus went to Galilee, full of the Spirit. After Galilee, He went to His hometown of Nazareth, and went into their synagogue on the Sabbath day, stood up and began to teach out of the book of Isaiah. He opened to a prophetic word about Himself and read:

> *The Spirit of the Lord is upon me, because he hath anointed me to preach the gospel to the poor; he hath sent me to heal the brokenhearted, to preach deliverance to the captives, and recovering of sight to the blind, to set at liberty them that are bruised, to preach the acceptable year of the Lord.* Luke 4:18-19

It was at this point, Jesus officially began His ministry. The Bible says God anointed Jesus with the Holy Ghost and power, and He went about doing good and healing all who were oppressed by the Devil. (Acts 10:38) The purpose of Jesus' ministry was to destroy the works of the Devil. (I John 3:8)

Now I want to show you something from the Word that will excite you. I John 3:1 says, "Behold what manner of love the Father hath bestowed upon

us, that we should be called the sons
we are the sons and daughters of (
mission as Jesus – to destroy the work

I want you to look at another verse

> But the anointing which ye h.
> you…

Praise God! We have the same anoi.
As He is, so are we in this world. He m.
hearted and preached deliverance to th
good and healing all who were oppressed
His name, brothers and sisters, and do the

…..Jiui in

…that exciting?

I can hear you thinking, "But, Pastor Nick, I've never felt any power like that in my life. Besides, I'm not called to the full-time ministry like you."

First of all, this anointing is for "all who believe." If you're a born again Christian, then you are anointed. And secondly, your "feelings" have nothing to do with whether you are anointed or not. The just shall live by faith. You believe you are anointed because the Bible says you are. Many times, when I pray for someone I don't "feel" God's anointing on me. But I know my *feeling* His power doesn't mean it's not there upon the person. We lay hands on people by faith, believing and standing on the promise of God's Word that we are anointed to destroy the works of the Devil in Jesus' name. Also, God's power won't manifest independent of His purpose. It is when you step out in faith to reach the lost for Jesus, that God's anointing will be manifest.

I'm always amazed how the anointing of God will prompt me to say the exact thing someone needs to hear. By the anointing, you will know what to say and how to handle every situation you encounter. In fact, I've been surprised at how the Holy Spirit will minister to people.

For instance, after I had been going down on the streets for a while, the spiritual gift of the word of knowledge began to operate through me – in an unusual way. I would approach someone and know instantly what their name was, or I would know what city and state they were from, or I would know something personal about them. I walked up to someone and said, "You're going through a divorce right now, aren't you?" Shocked they said, "How did you know?" I always tell them the Holy Spirit told me. It gets their attention real fast.

...usual experience regarding the manifestation of the ... was near a gas station and a man pulled up in a car. I ... and asked him if he wanted to hear some good news. He ... ly, "I don't want to hear it." I said okay, and started to back ... did, the Holy Spirit told me he was a Muslim. I said to him, ... a Muslim, aren't you?" He looked surprised and said, "How did you ...w?" I told him the Holy Spirit told me. Then the Holy Spirit told me he ...as from Somalia. Again, I said to him, "You're from Somalia, aren't you." He was even more surprised and asked again, "How did you know?" Again, I told him the Holy Spirit told me. A third time, the Holy Spirit told me what his name was. I said to the man, "Your name is Mohammed, isn't it?" This time the look on his face was incredulous. He demanded, "How do you know that?" I told him a third time, "The Holy Spirit told me."

I never did get to talk to him about the Lord, but I know that God does not manifest His gifts in vain. I'm confident there was a reason for God revealing those things about that man. He went away with plenty to think about. Most likely, he'll be more open to the next Christian who talks to him about Jesus. I'm sure of that.

Just in case, you're tempted to think this happens to me because I'm called to the five-fold office of evangelist, let me share a couple of testimonies from people in my ministry. One of our teams was in North Minneapolis when there happened to be a block party going on. Two of the people in their team, Summer and Jason, both had a word of knowledge that they would bump into someone they knew from high school or college and that they would be open for ministry. Summer said, "We had an expectancy that we would have a divine encounter with someone at least one of us knew. A while later, I heard someone call my name. It was a college student who worked at my office. She introduced me to her sister and best friend. They wanted to know what I was doing there, so I told them. All three of them prayed to receive Jesus."

Another girl from my ministry, Jennie, had an unusual experience. While on the bus, she and the other members in her team were praying. Jennie saw in her spirit a man wearing a brown coat and the face of a little girl. They arrived at their destination and were dropped off in a South Minneapolis neighborhood. They saw two girls standing on the street and went to talk to them. Jennie felt drawn toward a certain house on the block. She walked toward the house and, as she did, the family came out. It was a man and wife with three children. She approached them and talked to the father and found that he was already born again. Jennie then felt a prompting to pray for the little girls. She asked the father if she could pray with them, and he was very enthusiastic about it. She took their hands and prayed a simple prayer, being led of the Spirit. When she was done, she thanked the father and said goodbye. As she was walking away she thought one of the little girls looked familiar. Then it hit her. It was the face of the little girl she saw in her spirit when they were praying on the bus. She turned back to look at the father. Sure enough, his coat was brown.

The Holy Spirit will not only guide you what to say to someone, but He'll guide you in what to pray as well. Brad and Tom shared with me this experience they had one night. They approached a man who looked dazed and shaken up, to share with him the good news. He said, "Your friends already prayed for me." In a very excited manner, he went on to share with them his unusual experience. "After they prayed for me, I went up into this apartment building. I saw these two huge guys with guns walking down the hall. I turned around and started to head for the door to get out of the building. As I was going down the stairs, I heard gunshots behind me." Brad and Tom asked, "What did they pray for you?" He said, "They prayed that God's protection would be on me, and that He would watch over me. They prayed with me just five minutes before it happened." God's love was demonstrated to him in a powerful way.

God Needs Your Availability

God has provided you with everything you need to share the Gospel. He's provided you with His ability. He's given you His authority. And He has anointed you to preach the Gospel. Yet these things are useless unless you give to God the one thing He needs from you – your Availability. That is the fifth and last "A" of evangelism that I want to talk about.

Again, I don't share these things to condemn you, but rather to stir your heart into action. If you don't go, who will? Romans 10:14-15 says:

How then shall they call on him in whom they have not believed? and how shall they believe in him of whom they have not heard? and how shall they hear without a preacher? And how shall they preach, except they be sent? as it is written, How beautiful are the feet of them that preach the gospel of peace, and bring glad tidings of good things!

Yes, the Devil is out there. And the last thing he wants is for you to share your faith and destroy his kingdom. Yes, he will fight you every step of the way with fear and distractions and negative feelings. But, glory to God, Jesus defeated him 2000 years ago on the cross. We are not ignorant of his devices against us. When we expose his tactics and recognize his roadblocks, half the battle is won.

Listen, Satan cannot stop you from going out and speaking God's Word into someone's life, and he can't stop people from receiving that Word into their life. The only real weapons he has are fear and deception. The fact that we know this puts the Devil in great disadvantage. The most difficult thing about evangelism is "showing up." You have to put down the fear in your mind. You have to get your flesh under control when it would rather lie on the couch and watch TV all night. And you have to get over feeling insecure about not having the whole Bible memorized. Those are the most common tactics the Devil uses to keep Christians from witnessing.

Let me tell you a secret. When you get involved with evangelism, you get a whole lot of blessings in return. Your life will change so dramatically, you won't recognize yourself. Shy people turn into bold people. Depressed people become full of joy. People who feel they have nothing to live for, are filled with meaning and a mission.

A guy named Joe from my ministry shared with me how street witnessing has changed his life. Here is his testimony:

"Street witnessing started out as something I would do 'some day.' My reasons for not going were two-fold. First, I didn't feel I knew enough Bible. Second, every time I tried to talk about the Lord, it always turned into an argument. But my friend got me involved.

"Pastor Nick tells us that it is not our responsibility to get people saved – it is the Holy Spirit's job. Our job is simply to show up and go out. I said, 'I can do that.' I also learned how to talk with someone without it becoming confrontational. As I've been faithful to 'show up' and 'go out,' I have learned how to minister to people. It's exciting to experience the anointing of the

Holy Spirit. At times, words flow out of you like a preacher and the gifts of the Spirit operate through you. Nick tells us, 'As you go, you grow,' and it is so true. Witnessing is fun."

Here is a testimony from Diana on what street witnessing did for her life.

"Evangelism has revolutionized my life. I used to be very depressed, withdrawn, and beaten down. Shortly after I got involved in evangelism, that was reversed. Instead of being depressed, I have great joy. Some people even say I have great boldness now.

"Many times, the Holy Spirit has led me to approach someone who was going through the same things I was going through. The Holy Spirit would prompt me to minister to their need, and I would end up ministering to myself as well.

"So far, I have gone on missions trips to Peru, Mexico, New York, and Chicago. God has provided the finances for me to go every time. It's true, all you have to do is make yourself available and step out – God makes the way."

Now I want to share with you a testimony from a woman named Ruth.

"I became a part of the evangelism ministry because someone kept asking me to try it. I hated the thought of it. Besides I felt inadequate. I knew only one scripture – John 3:16. One day in front of several people, this person asked me to go out witnessing. I was too embarrassed to say no. I felt sort of trapped into it. That night when I drove to church, my flesh and mind were screaming, 'I DON'T WANT TO GO.'

"But I decided to try it at least three times. By the third time, I was filled with the Holy Spirit and my entire life has changed. God has taught me that if I am willing and obedient, I can be a witness anywhere. Witnessing is no longer a chore. It is imbedded within my soul."

Brothers and sisters, has your Christian experience become dull and boring? Has the fire gone out of your lamp? Has your relationship with God become routine? If it has, you need a shot in the arm. You need to begin sharing your faith. It will transform your life. You will start waking up in the morning glad to be alive. Your life will have purpose and meaning. And as you obey His command to "go," the desire to be used of God will be fulfilled.

Chapter Three

Evangelism…What Is It?

E·van·gel·ize (i-van´ je-liz) v. 1. To preach the gospel, 2. To convert to Christianity.

This is how the dictionary defines the word "evangelize" – a verb meaning to preach the Gospel or to convert to Christianity. But the Bible's definition of "evangelize" is much more than just a verb.

In Acts 26:17-18, Jesus commissioned the apostle Paul saying, "I am sending you, to open their eyes so that they may turn from darkness to light and from the dominion of Satan to God, that they may receive forgiveness of sins and an inheritance among those who have been sanctified by faith in Me." (NASV)

Evangelism is opening the eyes of the lost about the free gift of salvation that Jesus provided through His death on the cross. It's about rescuing people out of Satan's dominion and introducing them to the kingdom of God. It's helping the sinner receive and accept the forgiveness of his sins and to receive the inheritance that belongs to those who are sanctified in Jesus. Evangelism is helping the lost make a decision that they can live with for all eternity.

The apostle John says this about preaching the Gospel; "…that ye also may have fellowship with us: and truly our fellowship is with the Father, and with his Son Jesus Christ. (1 John 1:3)

Evangelism is about being so excited about the new life you're experiencing in Jesus that you want others to experience it too. So that they can also "have fellowship with the Father and with His Son Jesus Christ."

What evangelism is "not," is asking people to join a particular church or to change *religions*. Evangelism is not about shouting at people and telling them to repent. And evangelism is not condemning people for their sins or judging them for their lifestyle.

Each week my ministry teams and I talk with people who have heard enough about Jesus to know who He is and what He did, but when it comes to the matter of salvation, they are confused. This confusion is usually caused by a lack of teaching, wrong teaching, or because they've heard conflicting doctrines from different denominations.

It reminds me of the scripture in Rom 10:2-4, "For I bear them record that they have a zeal of God, but not according to knowledge. For they being ignorant of God's righteousness, and going about to establish their own righteousness, have not submitted themselves unto the righteousness of God. For Christ is the end of the law for righteousness to every one that believeth."

When we talk to people about Jesus, they have a "zeal for God, but not according to knowledge." They are ignorant of God's righteousness. They believe they are going to heaven because "I'm a good person," or they tell us, "I was confirmed in the church," or they tell us, "I was baptized as an infant," and believe it or not, we also hear this a number of times, "I've never killed anybody."

There are many people who are genuinely searching for the truth and all they need is someone to explain the scriptures to them so they can understand the way of salvation. They have willing and hungry hearts and they quickly embrace the truth when they hear it.

"Pastor Nick, you've convinced me of the need to evangelize, but I just don't think I can convince anybody to follow Jesus."

You're right. You can't convince anybody to follow Jesus. But God's Word in your mouth can. Paul said in 1 Cor 1:17-18, "For Christ sent me not to baptize, but to preach the gospel: not with wisdom of words, lest the cross of Christ should be made of none effect. For the preaching of the cross is to them that perish foolishness; but unto us which are saved it is the power of God."

When Paul preached the Gospel he knew that clever words would not get anybody saved. Paul preached the cross because the power of God was on that message. People aren't going to get saved because of how clever or how articulate you sound when you're witnessing. They get saved by the anointing and power of God that is on the Word you share with them. I've seen people stammer and stumble on their words when they first start out, and in spite of how nervous or inarticulate they were, God used them to lead people into salvation. It's not your responsibility to get people saved. That's

God's job. Your job is just to share the Good News. Always remember, the lost cannot get saved apart from the power of God.

"But Pastor Nick, what Word do I preach? I don't know where to start."

The first scripture our workers learn is Romans 10:9-10, "That if thou shalt confess with thy mouth the Lord Jesus, and shalt believe in thine heart that God hath raised him from the dead, thou shalt be saved. For with the heart man believeth unto righteousness; and with the mouth confession is made unto salvation."

This passage of scripture is literally all you need to know in order to lead someone to Jesus. Sure, it's good to put as much Word in your heart as possible so the Holy Spirit will have more to draw on, but many, many souls have been saved through this ministry by this passage alone.

It's Not Just for the Streets

Properly understood, evangelism is not something you do once a week when you go out with your church. (Or however many times you might go out.) Evangelism should be part of your everyday life – it's a lifestyle. You can be an evangelist every day.

People in my ministry become confident, bold, and increased with wisdom when they begin street witnessing, and this confidence helps them to share Jesus with their family, friends and coworkers. People discover that when they are faithful to go out on the streets to witness, God opens doors for them to share the Gospel throughout the week. They become more "evangelistically aware." It's truly exciting to be used of God anytime and anywhere to help someone get saved and often when you least expect it.

One time I was ministering in a church in Jacksonville, Florida. After the service, the pastor and some of the people from his church took me out to eat at a Shoney's restaurant. Our waitress was a 19-year-old girl named Shawna. We were full of the joy of the Lord, and all of us were laughing. When she came up to our table she made a comment about how happy we were. I held up my glass and asked if I could get a slice of lemon in my water. At that moment, the Spirit of God fell on Shawna and she started laughing with the rest of us. The anointing on her was so strong that she became hot and started to fan herself with the menu. She left to get me a lemon and when she came back, I said to her, "Shawna, I'm a pastor and I've been taking a survey. I'd like to ask you a question. If you died today, do you know for sure you'd go to heaven?" She gave me an emphatic "yes." I asked her, "What would be the reason you would go to heaven?" She said, "Because I'm a good person." I went on to explain to her that it's good to strive to be a good person, but the good news is, it's not by anything we do that gets us into heaven. It's what Jesus did on the cross and that we can't work our way into heaven. We talked a while and then I asked her if she would like to receive Jesus. The Spirit of God was on her so strong that she cried all through the prayer.

This is not an isolated incident. This happens to me and people in my ministry all the time. It's because evangelism is a lifestyle to us. And because of that, God sends people our way. In fact, at the writing of this book I prayed with three people at a fast-food restaurant yesterday and then at night I prayed with our waitress at a local restaurant. I believe that's how God wants all of us to live each day of our lives.

Like the apostle Paul said, we are to "Preach the word; be instant in season, out of season; reprove, rebuke, exhort with all longsuffering and doctrine." (2 Timothy 4:2)

We Each Have Unique Gifts

The Word says in Ephesians 4:16, "From whom the whole body fitly joined together and compacted by that which every joint supplieth, according to the effectual working in the measure of every part, maketh increase of the body unto the edifying of itself in love."

We all have a supply to give. Each of us giving our supply and using the gifts God has placed in us will get the job done. While I believe everyone in the body of Christ should go out on the streets at least occasionally, I realize that we are not all called to go to the streets specifically. Some of us are called to other forms of evangelism such as nursing homes, prisons, to the youth, or to a foreign mission field. It's my opinion that no matter where God has called you to minister, street evangelism is a good place to get the training you'll need. There are those in my ministry that started on the streets and God has used them to lead literally thousands to Christ on foreign missions fields. One man, named Troy, spent three months in Peru and while there, he prayed with over 10,000 people to receive Jesus.

Because we are all unique, some of us will find it easier to minister the Word of God using other forms or "methods" of evangelism. The Bible shows us several different ways in which we can share our faith. Let's look at a few.

One-On-One Evangelism

The first method I want to talk about (which is also the main focus for this book) is what I call, "one-on-one evangelism." Some people call it "confrontational evangelism," but I don't like that term because it seems to convey a negative connotation. It could be said that we do confront people with the decision to accept or reject Jesus as their personal Lord and Savior, but it's not done in an "in your face" confrontational manner. We do it in love and gentleness.

We approach people who are on the streets one-on-one or in small groups of usually three people. It's not unlike an evangelistic crusade or tent meeting, except that instead of the people going to the preacher, the preacher goes to them. An example of this type of evangelism is in the second chapter of Acts. It's right after Jesus ascended to Heaven and He told the disciples to tarry in the upper room in Jerusalem. You're familiar with what happened. It says in Acts 2:2, "…suddenly there came from heaven a noise like a violent rushing wind, and it filled the whole house where they were sitting." (NASV) Everyone in that upper room was filled with the Holy Spirit and began to speak in tongues.

People everywhere heard the noise and began to gather around wondering what was going on. So Peter jumped up and preached that Jesus is the Son of God and that He died and rose again to save all those that will accept Him as Messiah. Peter told them how to get saved and 3000 of them decided to receive the free gift of salvation.

That is a great example of approaching people on the street and sharing Jesus. But there are other forms or methods of evangelism that are both scriptural and effective.

Evangelism in Relationships

I've heard it said that family and friends are the hardest people to witness to. That's nonsense. You just have to have wisdom in how you share the Gospel with them. Obviously, the one-on-one approach probably wouldn't be the best way. The best way to win them to Christ is by building a trusting relationship with them and when the time is right (the Holy Spirit will prompt you), you can share Jesus with them.

Rather than a brief encounter on the streets, this form of witnessing takes place over a longer period of time. For that reason, it's vital you live what you preach, because they'll be watching you very closely. How you live your life will either be a powerful witness to them, or it will be an excuse not to believe the Word of God. As Christians, our lives should be a living epistle for all to observe.

Also, don't think you have to be the one to pray with a family member. That's pride. God knows exactly the right person to bring across their path to pray with them. If that's you, great! If not, who cares? What's important is that they get saved. It says in Acts 16:31, "Believe in the Lord Jesus Christ and thou shalt be saved and thy house." Praise God, you can stand on that promise and see your whole family come into the kingdom through you or someone else. What matters is that you're faithful to share the Word of God with them when the Holy Spirit prompts you.

Some think this method of evangelism is reserved only for family and friends, but don't ignore the other minor relationships in your life like waitresses in your favorite restaurant, the bank teller in your bank, gas-station attendants, and the like. Though you aren't close to any of these people, you do have somewhat of a relationship with them. In fact, anyone you do business with or encounter on a regular basis is a candidate for building a relationship in which to share Jesus with him or her.

Before I became full-time in the ministry, I worked in the post office. When I worked there, I ministered to a fellow employee named Nick and he got born again and started going to my church. Ten years later I went back to visit with all the Christians who worked there. (There were several.) I asked Nick if any of the other Christians ever approached him to talk about Jesus and he said no. That made me sad. Here this place was filled with Christians, who had the light and life of God in them and none of them reached out to their fellow employees with the Good News.

Every day we should live our lives with the knowledge that we are somebody's divine appointment, to introduce him or her to Jesus. We must be obedient to take advantage of the opportunities that come our way to share the love of God. We must!

Service Evangelism

Another form of evangelism is what is called, "service evangelism." An example of service evangelism is found in the story of the Good Samaritan in Luke 10. While traveling down a road, a good Samaritan came across someone with a need. He selflessly met that man's need. In the same way today, "random acts of kindness" will get a person's attention fast.

Every year our church's school has an event called "Operation: Good Samaritan." The children go into the homes of the poor and elderly who have great need and overwhelm them with the love of God by doing acts of kindness. They clean garages, mow lawns, rake yards, paint rooms, clean homes. Many of the people they minister to live in homes with no furniture. They have often furnished people with a whole room full of furniture. They supply beds, dishwashers, dressers, couches, dishes, clothing, toys, pots and pans... whatever the need is, they try to meet it.

The people are so overwhelmed they laugh and cry at the same time. They are truly overwhelmed with love. When the kids finish with their work, they share with them the most important gift of all – the free gift of salvation. Many people are won to the Lord on Operation: Good Samaritan day. When you reach out to meet someone's physical need, they are open to hear what you have to say.

Invitational Evangelism

Another way to get people saved is to simply invite them to come hear someone preach. Maybe there is someone you know who isn't receptive when you share the Lord with them. Yet those same people may soften in an atmosphere filled with the anointing and presence of God and will respond to the minister.

This is the method of evangelism the woman at the well used in John 4. Jesus talked with her at the well and He had a word of knowledge for her about her life. She was amazed by Jesus; the Bible says "The woman then left her waterpot, and went her way into the city, and saith to the men, Come, see a man, which told me all things that ever I did: is not this the Christ? Then they went out of the city, and came unto him." (John 4:28-30)

It says they "besought" Jesus to stay with them. He stayed in that city for two days and many people came to believe in Him simply because one person invited them to come "hear a man." Never underestimate how a simple invitation to come to church can affect someone's life. My pastor always makes sure that our church has special events going on so the members can invite their relatives to come to church. Baby dedication is a good one. The pastor always preaches a salvation message that Sunday because he knows many unsaved family members and friends will be there.

Sharing Your Testimony

Another powerful witnessing tool is the simple act of sharing your testimony. That's what the "madman" of the Gadarenes did and he influenced an entire city for Jesus. Most everyone is familiar with his story. Jesus came upon a man who was possessed with a legion of demons. Jesus cast them out and the demons entered into a herd of swine and they all ran into the sea and drowned. The people of the town became afraid of Jesus and asked Him to leave.

Later in the story, this man is so grateful for what Jesus did for him that he asked if he could go with Jesus and His disciples. It says in Mark 5:19-20, "Howbeit Jesus suffered him not, but saith unto him, Go home to thy friends, and tell them how great things the Lord hath done for thee, and hath had compassion on thee. And he departed, and began to publish in Decapolis how great things Jesus had done for him: and all men did marvel."

Jesus told this man to go home and share with his friends what the Lord had done for him. He did and it says they "all marveled." In the gospel of Luke, it says Jesus came back to that city and this time, they didn't ask Him to leave but instead received Him gladly. This happened because of one man's testimony.

Praise God, you can do the same as the madman of Gadera. Your story of how God delivered you from whatever you used to be in bondage to is powerful, especially to those who are in similar struggles. Many have given up all hope of ever being free and happy again. But when you can confidently tell them, "I understand what you're going through. Let me tell you how Jesus set me free and restored my life," you'll see hope return to their eyes. It's a perfect opportunity to tell them that there is a way out, and His name is Jesus.

Of course, there are more ways to evangelize than those I've listed here. As you use the God-given gifts that are in you, you'll develop your own "style" that works best for you. I think I should say here that evangelism should not be viewed as a "method." It sounds manipulative. Evangelism is a heartfelt desire to sow the incorruptible seed of God's Word into the hearts of the lost. No matter how you share the Gospel, as long as you're motivated by love and are led by the Holy Spirit, your labor will bear fruit for the kingdom of God.

Can God Count on You to Share Jesus?

When God knows He can count on you to preach and teach about Jesus to the lost, He'll start bringing people to you. It happens to my teams and me quite often. In fact, let me tell you about one of the most unusual ways God has led people to us.

Jake told me about an unusual experience he had. He called an old friend, Jenny, who he hadn't seen since he had gotten saved. He wanted to share Jesus with her. Jake began to share with Jenny that he had given his life to the Lord and how much his life had changed. Right in the middle of his testimony, Jenny interrupted him and said, "I have to tell you something. Last night, I had a dream about this phone call. Everything you've shared with me, I dreamed." Needless to say, Jenny received Jesus as her Lord.

I had a similar experience happen to me. I walked into the city center in downtown Minneapolis. I noticed a man walking toward me, looking at me very strangely. Just as he was about to pass by, he blurted out at me, "I know you." I didn't recognize him at all and I have a good memory for faces. I asked him, "Where are you from?" He said, "Arkansas." I told him, "I've never been to Arkansas."

He became insistent, "I know, I know you from somewhere. I've seen you before..."

"Sorry..." I replied.

Then his face lit up with recognition. He snapped his fingers and said, "I remember where I saw you! Believe it or not, but I saw you in a dream I had. You approached me and took me by the hand and led me through this tunnel. It was like a tunnel of light."

Right away I realized I was experiencing a divine encounter. I held out my hand to him and said, "I want to lead you to the light. His name is Jesus." He was overcome with emotion as he prayed the prayer of salvation with me.

Chapter Four

Love Never Fails

The most important thing I try to impart to people when they're out on the streets witnessing is that love never fails. Some people don't take it seriously enough. They respond flippantly, "Yeah, yeah, love never fails. I know, Pastor Nick."

It is vital you understand that love must be the foundation for all you do. When you give someone the good news of salvation, your motive for sharing has to be love. Even the apostle Paul said as much. In 1 Corinthians 13:3, "And though I bestow all my goods to feed the poor, and though I give my body to be burned, and have not charity, it profiteth me nothing."

Paul is saying here that your motive for Christian ministry must be love. If it isn't, it profits you nothing. Love is a powerful thing. It can melt the hardest of hearts. But it has to be genuine; you can't fake it. It's easy for people to recognize the real thing, and it's easy to detect insincerity too.

I'm sad to say much of the body of Christ has been going about evangelism the wrong way. Trust me, I've seen it. They're out there hitting people over the head with their Bibles, condemning them and pointing out their sins. Using scare tactics like, "If you don't repent, you're going to hell." Telling someone they're going to hell is pointless. The world doesn't have a true revelation of hell. It's just a fictional place to them. If they did have a true revelation of hell, they would instantly repent of their sins and get right with God in a second.

Judging and criticizing people will never draw them to Jesus. I remember this woman named Karen telling me about Bill. Bill loved God with all his heart. He had gotten saved out of the gangs in New York and moved to Minneapolis to start over. One day he looked kind of depressed, and Karen asked him what was wrong. Bill said he was discouraged because he had been going down on the streets of downtown Minneapolis witnessing and handing out tracts for ten years and hadn't prayed with one person. He couldn't understand his lack of success.

Then Karen told me she and some other Christians were going to a Christian coffee house one Saturday night. They saw Bill on the street corner with a stack of tracts in his hand talking to people as they passed by. She said, "We got up close enough to hear him. We were shocked by what he said to the passersby. He made up some kind of jingle-chant that sounded like, 'Hey all you sinners, wallowing in sin, clean up your act, meet Jesus, get out of your ole pig pen.' We were horrified. The mystery why he couldn't get anyone to pray with him was all too clear."

I heard another horror story when I was invited to minister at a church in Missouri about evangelism. The believers in that church told me about a group of deceived Christians who were a reproach to Christ. They went into populated areas and held up picket-like signs with messages on them that read, "Turn or Burn," or "Turn From Your Wicked Ways." Not surprisingly, they hadn't prayed with one person. These poor deceived people explained their lack of success by saying that the sinners didn't talk to them because they felt too convicted. What ignorance! Unfortunately, there are all too many people who have this mentality.

Loving the World

When you read the Gospels, you never see Jesus condemning anybody, coming down hard on their sin. In fact, the Bible says specifically that He didn't come to condemn. Look at John 3:17; "For God sent not his Son into the world to condemn the world; but that the world through him might be saved."

God didn't send Jesus into the world to condemn it, and neither did Jesus send us into the world to condemn it. He had great compassion for the world and, as a result, great multitudes were drawn to Him. If you are born again, that same love and compassion is in you, and it will draw great multitudes to Jesus.

Because I used to be an alcoholic, I was adamant about not being around it. I knew first hand how alcohol could destroy your life. I preached against it and was very condemning toward anyone who drank. My family was all too aware of my stand against alcohol. My heart's desire was to be righteous before the Lord, but I wasn't aware that I was coming off as *self-*righteous.

One day my wife Jane and I were driving in the car when the Lord spoke to me. I told Jane, "The Lord just told me He wants me to find my uncle today and talk with him." Jane said, "Where do you think he is?" I told her, "Most likely he's in a bar somewhere."

I made some calls and found out which bar he was at. We drove over and when I walked in the door, his eyes got big as saucers. He was shocked that I would come into a bar to talk with him. I sat down and right away he asked me, "Nick, can I order you a 7-up?" I told him, "No thanks, I just wanted to come visit with you and let you know how much I love you." We visited for a while and then Jane and I left.

A few months later, I learned how important it is to obey the leading of the Lord. I got a call from a family member telling me my uncle was in the hospital dying. I called up a friend, Pete, and he and I went to the hospital to minister him. I'm grateful to report that he received Jesus as his Lord and Savior. A short time later he passed away.

There is no doubt in my mind that my uncle was open to the message of salvation because of my obedience to seek him out a few months earlier. If I hadn't done that, I'm confident he wouldn't have received from me, thinking that I condemned him for his lifestyle. But I'm confident my visit to the bar eliminated those feelings. Love opened the door.

The message of love is able to stop people in their tracks – literally. I remember one experience my wife Jane and I had on a busy downtown street in Minneapolis. A UPS truck pulled up in front of a store and the driver got out of the truck with several packages in his arms. Jane and I walked up to him and I asked him, "Can I give you some good news?" He said, "No, I don't have time." As he walked away, I said to him, "Jesus loves you." He stopped instantly in his tracks, turned around, and came up to us and said, "Tell me about it." He prayed to receive Jesus, all the while holding his packages. Afterward, he thanked us and then went on his business. I always tell people that he got delivered and then he delivered his packages.

A girl named Diana from my ministry shared with me something she and her team witnessed one night during our regular Monday night evangelism. They saw a middle-aged man in a heated discussion with a small group of Christians (who were not with our group). He broke off from them, angrily shouting, "You're all just a bunch of fake Christians."

He headed straight for Diana and her team and they engaged him in conversation. It turns out these Christians refused to pray for his girlfriend because they were "living together." It took a while to get the facts of the story straight, but his girlfriend was really just his friend. She was a 70-year old woman who showed compassion on him when he was homeless and took him into her home. He said something was wrong with her mind and he just wanted someone to pray for her. This group of Christians thought they were living in sin and refused to pray with him. That's what caused this man to blow up in anger.

I want to share with you another sweet testimony one of my workers, Jeff, gave me. It was his very first experience street witnessing. He told me, "I was pretty pumped up, but after getting off the bus in a bad area of Minneapolis, reality hit me. I decided not to be discouraged. We set out and soon came to a Spanish speaking housing development. Jason and Summer felt led to go up to these two little boys playing in the front yard. In Spanish, Jason asked them if they knew Jesus. Just then, their father stuck his head out of a window from the second floor and shouted at us, 'What are you talking about to my boys?' We told him, 'Jesus.' His eyes lit up and he said, 'My name is Luis Diez and I want you to come into my house and tell me more about Jesus.' When we came into his home, he told us a very sad thing. He said, 'I have invited many people from many churches to my home to tell me the Word of God, but none have come. You are the very first to enter my home with the Word of God.' As Jason spoke with the father, Summer and I spoke with his 13-year-old daughter. She led his daughter in prayer and then gave her a Spanish Bible. Then Summer did something that almost brought me to tears. She felt led of God to take off her earrings and give them to the daughter. These were her most treasured earrings, given to her by her mother. I don't know who was more blessed by that, me or the little girl."

Love will never discriminate against a person for his or her status in life.

When you're on the streets doing the work of an evangelist, you'll see people living in obvious sin. It's tempting to look down your nose and pass judgment on an alcoholic, homeless person. But when you feel disgust rise in your heart, know this: while God hates their sin, He loves them as much as He loves you. Romans 5:8 says, "But God commendeth his love toward us, in that, while we were yet sinners, Christ died for us."

The only real difference between you and the drunk in the street is Jesus.

In a way, you can compare the lost to little children at play in the street, unaware they are in danger. Would anyone criticize or condemn those children for being in the street? Of course not. You would rush up to the children, scoop them up in your arms, and rescue them out of harm's way. That's how we need to approach the lost.

People are searching for the love of God and they aren't even aware of it. They have a big empty hole in their heart and they try to fill it up with sex, drugs, alcohol, gangs, and the like. Of course, God can only fill that hole. Ecclesiastes 3:11 says, "He [God] has put eternity in their hearts…" They're looking for the love of God in all the wrong places, but when they come in contact with the real thing, they instantly respond to it.

When I approach the lost, I always tell them that God loves them. The lost need to hear that God loves them. People have been told God is mad at them and He will make them pay for their sin with eternal hell. Think about that for a moment. If you were lost, would that cause you to draw near to God? Have you ever seen a child willingly run to an angry parent they know is going to scold him? Of course not. Why then do we think the lost will run to an angry God who is only going to throw them in hell?

Many people I talk to know the sin in their lives is wrong, and they already feel condemned about it. They want to be reconciled to God, but they think they have to clean up their lives before they can come to God. Or they think their lives are too messed up for God to love them. It's good news to them to learn God loves them just like they are and that He wants to free them from bondage. They just need someone to show them The Way.

We must portray a true picture of our heavenly Father – arms wide open, longing for the lost to receive His embrace of love through Jesus' salvation.

We Are to Reflect Jesus' Love

What do you do if you lack a genuine love for the lost? Ask God for a revelation of how He sees them. With a revelation of His love, when you see a drunk, a drug dealer, a gang member, or a prostitute, you won't see them as such. Instead, you'll see a brother or sister in bondage to the forces of darkness, who are unknowingly headed down a path which is destined for the lake of fire for all eternity.

The Bible says in Matthew 5:16, "Let your light so shine before men, that they may see your good works, and glorify your Father which is in heaven."

Unbelievers need to see us walking in love, doing our best to imitate Jesus. People have their guard up, because we live in a culture that takes advantage of others. Many have been hurt so often that they don't trust anyone. Not even God. It's tough to penetrate that hardness of heart. But love, true Christ-like love, can do it. When someone realizes you're not trying to get them to change religions and join your church, or try to force your opinions of God on them, they're open to hear what you have to say.

One of the laborers in my ministry, Mark, learned about the power of love during his first attempt at witnessing. He had only been saved a few months when one evening he went to see his childhood friend, Tim, with the intent of leading him to Jesus. These men had been best friends for 33 years, since they were 4 years old. Tim was his best man at his wedding and is the godfather to his youngest daughter.

They grew up in the same denominational church, so he knew that his friend already believed in Jesus. After four hours of discussion, scripture reading, and heated debate, Tim refused to pray. Mark said he could tell Tim understood the message, he simply refused to surrender his traditional beliefs. Finally at about 1:30 in the morning, Mark gave up the argument and, in defeat, laid his head on the kitchen table. He was emotionally and mentally exhausted from the long debate and couldn't think of anything else to say.

From this defeated position, Mark looked up and said, "Tim, you are my best and closest friend that I have in the world. I just want to make sure that you'll be in heaven with me some day. That's all." At that, Tim picked up the salvation prayer that had been before him all night and prayed to receive Jesus.

What happened? Love! When Tim realized his friend wasn't trying to convince him that his beliefs were all wrong, but instead was only concerned about his eternal destination, it broke down his defensive barriers.

Be Persistent

Love never gives up on people. We take our teams into the same areas of the city week after week. There are people that we see every time we go out. And we witness to them every single week. And every week, they tell us they don't want to pray. But that never stops us from asking them again next week. You never know, their lives can change drastically in just one week and the next time you see them, they might have a change of heart.

Two examples come to my mind right away. One is about a man named Thomas, who we always encountered at the same time waiting for the bus. We faithfully witnessed to this man every time we saw him and he wouldn't even take a tract from us. Finally, one day five years later when we approached him one night, he was ready to listen. Thomas ended up praying to receive Jesus. Praise God!

Kay, a newcomer to the evangelism ministry, just recently came up to me and shared with me her testimony. She told me that sixteen years ago she was standing on Hennepin Avenue and I came up to her and asked her if she wanted to hear some good news. She blew me off and said, 'I'm okay.' I offered her a tract but she wouldn't take it. She said that I talked to her every week, and every week she blew me off. But all the seed I had planted in her heart had an effect and one day she became a Christian. She said I never came off condemning and that I always smiled. Three years after we witnessed to her, she visited our church and is now a member! And not only that, she comes out with us street witnessing! I didn't know that until she told me. I never cease to be amazed at what God does.

LWCC All Church Evangelism

*Street witnessing in the
middle of the winter in
Minneapolis, MN*

*Jane and I
ministering in Peru*

Peru, deaf lady healed

*Howard got saved in
Los Angels during a city blitz*

*Healed immediately from a broken
arm in the jungle city of Iquitos, Peru*

*Deaf man healed
in Costa Rica*

Nick and Jane in Iquitos, Peru

City blitz in Washington D.C.

Street witnessing in Peru

Roxanne ministering in Costa Rica

Teaching at an Evangelism Seminar in St. Paul, MN

Policemen in Costa Rica prayed to receive Jesus

Healing Crusade in Lima, Peru

Arequipa, Peru 2,100 Kids saved at Parochial School

Talking to former President of Costa Rica

Team prayer in Iquitos, Peru

Women healed in Arequipa, Peru

Teaching in Iquitos, Peru

Sharing Jesus on the streets in Kanas City

Ministering to a woman in Peru

*Policemen in Costa Rica
prayed to receive Jesus*

Ministering in Peru

*Prayed with man to receive Jesus in
market place in Costa Rica*

Nick praying with man on the streets

Nick praying with man to receive Jesus

Street witnessing in Peru

Chapter Five

Why People Don't Evangelize

I find that most Christians *desire* to lead others to Christ. They want to see the lost delivered and set free from the powers of darkness. Yet, few Christians in the body of Christ are actively sharing their faith with others. And even fewer churches have regular evangelistic outreaches.

Why is that?

The answer is obvious. We have an adversary, Satan, who is actively doing everything possible to prevent people from being born again into the kingdom of God. Yet when Jesus died on the cross and went to hell, He stripped Satan of all power and authority. How is it then that Satan is still able to prevent believers from spreading the Good News?

He does it through the only tool he has – deception.

Satan has no power to keep you from sharing the Good News with the lost. And he has no power to prevent the lost from accepting Jesus as their Lord and Savior. The only weapon he has in his arsenal is to get "you" to "choose" not to share Jesus. He does that through lies. He has a long list of lies and excuses he uses. Which of the following has he used on you?

"You've got things to get done tonight that just can't wait any longer."

"The way you acted today, you're not worthy to go out and share Jesus."

"You haven't been saved long enough. You're not qualified to witness."

"You don't know enough Bible. What if somebody asked you something about the Bible and you don't have the answer"?

"You shouldn't go out tonight. You worked so hard today, you really should go to bed early or you'll be wiped out for work tomorrow."

"You don't have the personality type to go out street witnessing."

Sound familiar?

The number-one tactic Satan uses against the believer is "fear of man." There are many variations of the fear theme. It could be fear of rejection. Fear of not performing as well as the others in your group. Or fear for your personal safety. But no matter what form fear takes in your life, you need to recognize that fear – all fear –does not come from God. The Bible says in 2 Timothy 1:7, "For God hath not given us the spirit of fear; but of power, and of love, and of a sound mind."

How Do We Deal With Fear?

How do we deal with this spirit of fear? First of all, you should understand the mechanics of fear, how it works. Fear is faith in reverse. In other words, fear is believing the Devil's lies, while faith is believing the truth of God's Word. In the same way that faith is increased by yielding to and acting on God's Word, fear is increased when you believe and yield to the Devil's lies. It's a matter of either yielding to God or yielding to Satan. The enemy wants you to yield to his fear because that transforms into bondage. He wants fear to be so strong in you that you'll never make a move to share your faith with others. When that happens, he's got you right where he wants you. Inactive. Harmless. Accomplishing nothing.

The battle of fear takes place in the arena of your mind. The battle is whether you yield to the lie or fight against it. The Bible says in Proverbs 23:7, "For as he thinketh in his heart, so is he..." That means if you think you can't witness to the unsaved about Jesus, then you probably won't. But if you think you can, then you most likely will.

Like I said, fear starts in your mind with a thought – a lie. *I can't do that. They might laugh in my face.* The next step is speaking the lie out of your mouth. "I can't do that. They might laugh in my face." Then that lie is carried out through your behavior – you end up staying home instead of going out witnessing.

Somebody famous once said about negative thoughts: "You can't do anything about the birds that fly over your head, but you can prevent them from building a nest in your hair." What he meant is that the Devil will speak lies to you, but you don't have to listen to them.

How then do we refuse negative thoughts from building a nest in our minds? By renewing our mind with the Word of God. In order to deal with the spirit of fear, you must first deal with the thoughts of fear. Look what the Bible says about thoughts:

> For though we walk in the flesh, we do not war after the flesh:(For the weapons of our warfare are not carnal, but mighty through God to the pulling down of strong holds;) Casting down imaginations, and every high thing that exalteth itself against the knowledge of God, and bringing into captivity every thought to the obedience of Christ," 2 Corinthians 10:3-5.

The Devil will speak lies to you. When he does, don't claim them. How do we claim them? It says in Matthew 6:31, "Therefore take no thought, saying…" You claim thoughts by "saying" them.

When negative thoughts come, you must cast them down and bring them captive to the obedience of Christ. For instance, when the thought of fear comes, *I can't do that. They might laugh in my face.* You must cast it down. Say out loud, "No! That's a lie. The Bible says I can do all things through Christ who strengthens me."

It's important you speak out loud – not think in your mind – the Word of God. Do this each time fearful thoughts come to your mind. Soon you'll notice these lies will come fewer and far between. Don't stop renewing your mind with the Word of God until every lie is gone.

I've prepared a list of scriptures you can begin speaking to yourself. A good idea would be to write them down on a piece of paper and carry them with you so they're convenient when you need them.

Psalms 118:6, "The Lord is on my side; I will not fear: what can man do unto me?"

Psalms 27:1, "The Lord is my light and my salvation; whom shall I fear? the Lord is the strength of my life; of whom shall I be afraid?"

1 John 4:4, "Ye are of God, little children, and have overcome them: because greater is he that is in you, than he that is in the world."

Proverbs 28:1, "The wicked flee when no man pursueth: but the righteous are bold as a lion."

1 John 4:18, "There is no fear in love; but perfect love casteth out fear: because fear hath torment. He that feareth is not made perfect in love."

Isaiah 26:3, "Thou wilt keep him in perfect peace, whose mind is stayed on thee: because he trusteth in thee."

Romans 10:11-12, "For the scripture saith, Whosoever believeth on him shall not be ashamed. For there is no difference between the Jew and the Greek: for the same Lord over all is rich unto all that call upon him."

James 4:7, "Submit yourselves therefore to God. Resist the devil, and he will flee from you."

"All right, all right, Pastor Nick. As soon as I drive the spirit of fear out of me and become bold, I'll go out witnessing."

Oops! You've just fallen for another lie from the enemy's dirty bag of tricks. Dealing with the spirit of fear is a two-fold process. First you control your thoughts and then you act against them. You act against them by doing the very thing fear is telling you not to do. Go out witnessing. Face it head on. Speak to that spirit of fear and tell it that it can't stop you. Then go out and walk through it. You'll most likely start out in fear, but each time you go out, fear will begin to dissipate until one day, it won't have any effect on you at all.

When that day comes, you've succeeded at renewing your mind like it says in Romans 12:2, "And be not conformed to this world: but be ye transformed by the renewing of your mind…"

This is a process all Christians must go through. We must train ourselves to listen only to the voice of the Good Shepherd. If you don't take fearful thoughts captive, they'll end up taking you captive and prevent you from fulfilling God's plans for your life.

Let me say this as well. The Bible calls Satan the "father of all lies." He never tells the truth. Everything he says is a lie. So when he tells you that you can't do something, then take that as a confirmation that you can and that he sees you as a threat to his kingdom.

You're Not Alone

Another element in confronting fear is being aware that you are not alone. When I first went out on the streets witnessing, some angry guy tossed a whiskey bottle at me from his car as he drove by. It missed me and it kind of frightened me a little. How I combated that fear was to start developing in myself the knowledge that I wasn't walking the streets by myself because God was with me. I constantly reminded myself that God was at my side every step. I used to read the scripture in Isa 41:10-13:

Fear thou not; for I am with thee: be not dismayed; for I am thy God: I will strengthen thee; yea, I will help thee; yea, I will uphold thee with the right hand of my righteousness. Behold, all they that were incensed against thee shall be ashamed and confounded: they shall be as nothing; and they that strive with thee shall perish. Thou shalt seek them, and shalt not find them, even them that contended with thee: they that war against thee shall be as nothing, and as a thing of nought. For I the Lord thy God will hold thy right hand, saying unto thee, Fear not; I will help thee.

You, too, need to develop a consciousness that God is with you, leading you, helping you, and teaching you every time you go forth in His name. Having this knowledge will bring comfort and confidence to your heart and mind.

Increase in Wisdom

Ephesians 4:15 says, "But speaking the truth in love, may grow up into him in all things, which is the head, even Christ." As you go, you grow. The more you share your faith, you will grow in experience and wisdom.

I encourage everyone new to evangelism to go out with others who have been doing it for a long time. Proverbs 13:20 says, "He that walketh with wise men shall be wise."

In the same way you learn by listening to your pastor teach the Word, you can learn by going out with experienced evangelists. You don't have to start out from "scratch" like I did. Take advantage of their wisdom. The first few times, just watch and listen. When you feel you're ready, step out.

If your church doesn't have an organized evangelistic outreach, then find a group of believers who are bold for Jesus and who are actively sharing their faith and ask if you can join them.

Increase in Boldness

Like I've said before, the hardest thing about evangelism is making up your mind to do it, and the second hardest thing is to keep doing it. Once you stand against the spirit of fear and start going out on the streets witnessing, rest assured, the Devil will bombard you with all sorts of lies to discourage you so that you'll quit. You might be attacked with condemning thoughts telling you that you're not doing it right, or that you're not making any difference so why bother going out anymore, or that you're actually making it worse for some.

One of Satan's most common lies is this: After you walk away from someone who didn't pray with you, he'll start bombarding your mind with thoughts like, *If you had said this, they would have prayed, or If one of the other more mature Christians had talked with them, they would have accepted the Lord.*

Don't listen to these lies for one second. You have to trust that the anointing of God was on what you said. Perhaps all you were supposed to do was plant a seed or water the seed someone else had planted in their heart. The Bible says "one plants, one waters, and God gives the increase." The next person to witness to them might be the one who harvests the crop.

One evening I approached a man who I had seen on the streets for many years. I walked up to him and began to talk with him. He said, "You guys have been out here doing this for 10 years." I said, "You're close. It's actually been 11 years." I began to share with him about the Lord and asked if he wanted to make Jesus his lord. He replied, "I really appreciate what you're doing, but I'm not ready right now." I gave him a hug and told him that Jesus loved him and that I'd pray for him.

At the end of the night when we were back at the church, I shared with the others about this man, how he had been watching us for 11 years on the street. I said I talked with him but he didn't want to pray right then. Someone from a different team than I had been with, popped up and said excitedly that his team had prayed with him to receive Jesus later in the evening. Praise God! One plants. One waters. But God gives the increase.

It's important to understand that just because someone doesn't pray with you, doesn't mean the truth you shared with him or her had no eternal effect.

Lie: You're Too Messed Up to Be Used of God

Another tactic the enemy uses against the believer is to get them involved in some kind of sin and then condemn them for it, causing them to lose their confidence in God. When I say "sin," I'm not talking about simply losing your temper or smarting off to someone. We know that when we mess up, we can claim I John 1:9, "If we confess our sins, he is faithful and just to forgive us our sins, and to cleanse us from all unrighteousness."

You confess the sin, repent of it, forget it, and go on. Of course, the enemy will try to magnify these mistakes and condemn you for them, but you must cast these thoughts down immediately. You know from the Word that you are in right standing with God.

The kind of sin activity I'm talking about is some kind of ongoing, unrepented sin, something that has become a stronghold in your life. And it's not necessarily the "big" stuff like adultery, fornication, drunkenness or the like. But it can be issues like ongoing anger, bitterness, or resentment toward someone. When sin like this is never dealt with, a believer will begin to lose their confidence toward God. They feel so condemned in their heart that they lose confidence to share their faith with others, or to minister on any level for that matter. It's hard to talk about God's forgiveness when you're wrestling with unforgiveness in your own heart.

The Devil will take advantage of your sin to condemn you and make you feel unworthy before God, so you'll hide from His presence in the same way Adam hid in the Garden of Eden.

Also, this kind of unrepented sin is especially damaging to your witness with your family and friends. They know you're a Christian so they're going to be watching you closely. The apostle Paul tells us in 2 Corinthians 3:2 that we are epistles known and read of all men. Therefore we need to avoid even the appearance of evil. We don't want our behavior to be a stumbling block to their salvation. They need to see something different about your life. They need to see something in you that they want for their own life.

61

Do you really live what you preach? Or are you a hypocrite?

When I worked at the Post Office, there was an unsaved man named Mitch who said to me one day, "Nick, I've been watching you for years and you really have changed, haven't you? I want to quit drinking like you did, Nick. Do you think God can change me like He did you?" Praise God! I shared the Word with him and he got saved. A year later, I heard that Mitch died and went home to be with the Lord. I thank God I lived a consistent life before him because it influenced him to want to change and accept Jesus.

If you have sin in your life that is ongoing, you need to deal with it so it doesn't affect your testimony before men. If you repent of it but keep slipping back into the same sin over and over, then perhaps you should seek counseling from your church. Get this issue settled in your life. Don't let it fester to the point you lose your confidence in God. And above all, don't allow your sin to be an excuse not to share your faith. Repent of it, get free, and go on.

One last thing along these lines: perhaps there are things in your past that you feel very ashamed about. So ashamed that the Devil has been beating you up about it. Well, rest assured, you're not the only person who has done some pretty lousy things in your past. Embrace the truth in Isaiah 54:4, "Fear not; for thou shalt not be ashamed: neither be thou confounded; for thou shalt not be put to shame: for thou shalt forget the shame of thy youth."

According to God, your past is forgiven. Don't even say God can't use you because of your past. It's all been washed away by the blood of Jesus. The Bible says "old things have passed away; behold, all things have become new" (2 Corinthians 5:17). In fact, your testimony of how God delivered you from your past can be a powerful witness and instrumental in bringing someone into the kingdom of God.

Pursue Boldness

Once you've overcome whatever fear might be preventing you from sharing your faith, don't stop there – keep going. Pursue the boldness of God. Start confessing scriptures about boldness (Ephesians 3:12; Romans 8:37; I Corinthians 15:57) and believe God for boldness to increase every time you go out on the streets witnessing. Expect and have confidence that people will pray with you to receive Jesus, or the baptism of the Holy Spirit, or healing or whatever they need from God.

A spirit of boldness will lead you into some powerful and exciting adventures with the Holy Spirit. Two laborers from my ministry, Mike and his wife Kelly, had a very exciting adventure. They were at a shopping mall witnessing. Mike said he felt the Holy Spirit tugging him to go into a women's department store. He said, "It's definitely not the first place I would go, but I obeyed the Holy Spirit's leading."

They met a young man named John and started to share Jesus with him. John said he believed in God and Jesus as a man, but he didn't believe in the death and resurrection of Jesus, nor did he believe that the miracles in the Bible actually happened. He simply didn't believe in the power of God.

Mike and Kelly shared with John from an intellectual perspective to the credibility of the Bible. He was open and received what they were saying. It was obvious that he was being ministered to by the Holy Spirit. They continued and explained mankind's need for a Savior. When they asked him if he'd like to receive Jesus, he was eager to pray with them.

After the prayer, they exhorted John in the faith and Mike ended the conversation. He shook hands with John and congratulated him on his new life in God. But John wouldn't let go of Mike's hand, and for about three minutes held on. Mike said, "I could tell he was receiving from God, so I just kept ministering to him about the Lord. When I finally let go of his hand, he took a deep breath and then fell flat on his back – slain in the spirit – right in the women's section in a department store."

He landed under a rack of women's blazers. Mike kneeled down beside John and pushed the blazer's out of his face and kept ministering to him. Said Mike, "The power of God was so strong on him, that I was tingling all over just sitting next to him. I asked him if anything like this had happened to him before. He couldn't speak and just shook his head 'no' at me." Mike explained it was the power of God and not to be afraid, that God was doing something very special in him.

They were just across from a checkout counter. One by one, three of the clerks came over at different times to check out the commotion. Mike reassured them everything was all right. To his surprise, they all left. A few minutes passed and John got up but he was still quite wobbly. Mike and Kelly helped him to a nearby chair. Praise God, John now believed in the power of God and, as a result, he received the baptism in the Holy Spirit with the evidence of speaking in tongues.

Brothers and sisters, it takes boldness to be used of God in that way. Wouldn't you like to have experiences like that? You can. Pray and believe God to help you get rid of fear and be filled with His boldness so you can do exploits for God, too.

Chapter Six

What About Follow-Up?

When my pastor caught wind of the success we were having on the streets, he asked me if I would be willing to head up the church's evangelistic outreach. He didn't have to ask me twice. Right away, I organized three weekly evangelistic outings for church members to participate in. People got involved right away, and God blessed our efforts. We had great success and many people prayed to receive Jesus. To God be the glory!

All through this time, the Devil had used every dirty trick in his bag to get me to stop, but I never did. So he took a different route – a sneak attack. He blindsided me by using my brothers and sisters in the Lord, causing me to second guess what I was doing. It caught me off guard and I didn't know how to respond… at first.

Christians began to come up to me in church and ask in a critical tone, "What are you doing about follow-up with all those people you pray with on the streets?" I'd say, "What do you mean?" They argued, "If you don't follow up on how they're doing, the Devil is going to eat their lunch. You can't just 'love 'em and leave 'em.' You've got to stay in contact with them and make sure they're learning and growing in God."

That threw me for a loop. We had prayed with literally hundreds of people by that time and I didn't know how we were ever going to make sure each and every one of them became mature Christians.

What's more, I had Christians come up to me and tell me that the people we were praying with were actually "false salvations." They claimed that they were not really getting saved because there was no sign of repentance, that they prayed with us too easily. I was floored by all of this criticism. I'm not ashamed to tell you, it hurt. And I cried a few tears about in it prayer to the Lord.

All the criticism made me start to second-guess what I was doing on the streets. I wondered if people really meant it when they prayed the prayer of salvation. They appeared to be sincere, but now I wasn't sure. Since it would be impossible to follow up on every person we prayed with, I began to wonder if what we were doing was right. Should I stop?

I wallowed in this self-doubt for a while, and then one day I finally came to my senses. Didn't Jesus command all Christians to go into all the world and preach the Gospel to every creature? And wasn't that what I was doing? And wasn't that what He called me to do?

God gave me a revelation that drew back the curtain of doubt and indecision and I was finally able to recognize the Devil's insidious attack for what it was. After that, I threw off the criticism and went forth confidently, doing the will of God, preaching the Gospel to every creature.

Also, I noticed something interesting about the people who criticized. Very few of them were involved in any kind of evangelistic effort at all. When I realized that, it got me steamed. Eventually, all the criticism died down. Only occasionally do I hear the follow-up question. Now when anybody criticizes, "What are you doing about follow up?" I simply ask them right back, "What are you doing about witnessing?" They simply walk away.

Every Member Does Its Part

During the height of all this pressure, I felt overwhelmed by how much ministry there was to do in our city, let alone our nation and the world. My thoughts were, "How can I possibly stay in contact with and follow up with each and every person we've prayed with? I'm only one person." The burden of seeing so much need and knowing there was only so much I could do, started to feel like a terrible weight.

I sought the Lord about this in prayer, and He began to minister to me about what His expectations were for me. And, as a result, He lifted the weight of the world from off my shoulders. Let's begin by looking at the following scriptures:

And he gave some, apostles; and some, prophets; and some, evangelists; and some, pastors and teachers; For the perfecting of the saints, for the work of the ministry, for the edifying of the body of Christ... From whom the whole body fitly joined together and compacted by that which every joint supplieth, according to the effectual working in the measure of every part, maketh increase of the body unto the edifying of itself in love. Ephesians 4:11,16.

For as we have many members in one body, and all me the same office: So we, being many, are one body in Chris members one of another. Having then gifts differing accord that is given to us, whether prophecy...or ministry... or ʟᴇᴀᴄʜɪɴɢ... exhortation... he that giveth... he that ruleth... he that sheweth mercy... Romans 12:4-8.

The collective body of Christ is made up of individuals who each have their own unique gifts and calling. Here we see the ministry callings are made up of apostles, prophets, evangelists, pastors and teachers. All ministerial, yet each office is different from the others in that its calling focuses on a particular kind of ministry. God doesn't expect the evangelist to do the work of the pastor or the teacher, or vice versa. He expects the evangelist to operate under the anointing of the evangelist, which is saving souls.

Romans chapter 12 describes our unique callings very succinctly. Though we are many members in the body of Christ, we don't all function in the same office or ministry. Here it lists a few offices – prophecy, ministry (serving), teaching, exhortation, giving, ruling (administrative) and showing mercy. We're all called of God to minister, but we're not cookie-cutter Christians. We're not all the same – or minister all the same.

I know what I'm telling you isn't an earth-shattering revelation. It's a very basic concept in Christianity, something you probably already know. All I'm trying to point out is that there is no such thing as a "one-man show" in the body of Christ. There is no such Christian who is a "jack of all trades" as far as ministry is concerned. Jesus is the only person on the earth who walked in full measure of the Holy Spirit (John 3:34). Every Christian has a "supply" that he is responsible to give. God only expects you to be faithful in giving the supply you have to give. He doesn't expect you to "do it all." He just wants you to be faithful to do your "part."

The Lord reassured me that He didn't expect me to be a "one-man show" for Him. His only expectation of me was to be faithful to the office He called me to – evangelist. My pastor has an excellent teaching on the five-fold ministry offices. He describes the office of the evangelist as being on the "front lines" of what God's doing in the earth. It's an exciting ministry.

The word *evangelist* means "one who brings glad tidings." The evangelist preaches about the salvation of Jesus Christ. This message is all the evangelist can focus on. He is consumed by it. It doesn't matter how badly he wants to teach on something else, his messages always end up focusing on the subject of salvation. If he starts talking about marriage, he'll wind up preaching about salvation. If he tries to preach about healing, it will come back to getting people saved. He majors on salvation. That's his calling.

There was an evangelist that Pastor told us about as an example of someone trying to minister outside his calling. He said a particular evangelist became inspired by someone who stood in the office of teacher. He decided to mold his ministry around this man and tried to teach messages on topics other than salvation. But every time he tried, the anointing on him lifted. His anointing lifted because God called him to the office of evangelist, not teacher. Although this man knew he was called to the office of evangelist, he wanted to flow in a different anointing. And it cost him the anointing of God. It is imperative to the plan of God that we do what He has called us to do.

The Collective Ministry Effort

The Holy Spirit is like a conductor leading his orchestra in playing a beautiful symphony. We, the body of Christ, are the orchestra. Though the orchestra is made up of many individuals who play different instruments, we operate together as one. What would happen if certain members of the orchestra refused to heed the direction of the conductor? The symphony would be a disaster.

That's the way it is on the streets. Everyone has a part to play in getting people saved. It's a cooperative effort. The Holy Spirit might have you plant a seed in someone and then someone else will come in and reap the harvest. This is what it means in the scripture in 1 Corinthians 3:6-10:

> I have planted, Apollos watered; but God gave the increase. So then neither is he that planteth any thing, neither he that watereth; but God that giveth the increase. Now he that planteth and he that watereth are one: and every man shall receive his own reward according to his own labour. For we are labourers together with God: ye are God's husbandry, ye are God's building. According to the grace of God, which is given unto me, as a wise masterbuilder, I have laid the foundation, and another buildeth thereon.

Every time you pray with someone to receive Jesus, you are the follow-up to the faithful workers who planted the seed of God's incorruptible seed in their heart. One person lays the foundation and another person comes along and builds upon it. They did their part and you did your part. What makes us think we can or should take responsibility for a person's entire salvation experience? It's not possible.

I'll share a touching testimony that illustrates how the body of Christ works together in unison when directed by the Holy Spirit. One of my workers, Mark, told me about this experience. He said, "We were downtown witnessing and that's where we met Hank. He told us he had been married for 10 years and had a 6-year-old son. His wife threw him out because of his drinking and cheating. Hank moved in with his mother who is a born again Christian. He told us that, that morning he was depressed about the way his life was going and talked to his mother about it. The only advice she gave him was, 'Hank, you need to turn your life over to the Lord.' He knew it deep down, but didn't do anything about it. He got on the bus and went to work and talked to his cousin Ernie, who had just gotten out of a drug and alcohol treatment center. While there, he got saved and was now on fire for Jesus. Hank opened up to Ernie about his life and Ernie gave him the same counsel his mother gave him. 'Hank, you need to turn your life over to the Lord.'

"This is where we come in. We approached Hank when he was waiting for his bus. We talked to him about the Lord and he prayed with us almost immediately. With tears streaming down his face, he told us about his life and then said, 'I always knew God was real, but I never knew that He loved *me,* but because of all the people He sent to me today, I know He loves me.'"

Isn't that a beautiful illustration of how the body of Christ works together in unison, being led by the Holy Spirit? One plants. One waters. And another reaps the harvest.

Did Philip Follow-Up?

Now I want to show you something about the experience of Philip the evangelist in Acts 8:26-40:

> And the angel of the Lord spake unto Philip, saying, Arise, and
> go toward the south unto the way that goeth down from Jerusalem

unto Gaza, which is desert. And he arose and went: and, behold, a man of Ethiopia, an eunuch...Was returning, and sitting in his chariot read Esaias the prophet. Then the Spirit said unto Philip, Go near, and join thyself to this chariot. And Philip ran thither to him, and heard him read the prophet Esaias, and said, Understandest thou what thou readest? And he said, How can I, except some man should guide me? ... Then Philip opened his mouth, and began at the same scripture, and preached unto him Jesus. And as they went on their way, they came unto a certain water: and the eunuch said, See, here is water; what doth hinder me to be baptized? And Philip said, If thou believest with all thine heart, thou mayest. And he answered and said, I believe that Jesus Christ is the Son of God. And he commanded the chariot to stand still: and they went down both into the water, both Philip and the eunuch; and he baptized him. And when they were come up out of the water, the Spirit of the Lord caught away Philip, that the eunuch saw him no more: and he went on his way rejoicing. But Philip was found at Azotus: and passing through he preached in all the cities, till he came to Caesarea.

Here we see the Holy Spirit doing His part as conductor. He directs Philip to travel south to Gaza and then he directs him to approach the eunuch and minister Jesus to him. Philip does his part and wins him to the Lord. Then I want you to see something very interesting. After Philip baptized the Eunuch, it says that the Holy Spirit caught Philip away and he never saw that man again.

What about the follow-up? Why didn't the Holy Spirit instruct Philip to stay with the Eunuch until he was able to give him proper follow-up? The Bible doesn't tell us if the Eunuch ever received any follow-up, but we know for sure he didn't get any from Philip.

Philip's experience with the Eunuch is the style of evangelism that we commonly refer to as street evangelism. Our critics call this the "love 'em and leave 'em" style of evangelism. They insist that if you aren't willing to follow up with them, becoming their personal mentor making sure they become mature in Christ, then you shouldn't pray with them to start with.

That is the most ridiculous thing I've ever heard of in my life. It would be the same as a doctor who refused to deliver a baby because he wasn't able to be a part of that baby's life, to make sure it was raised properly. How many of you agree that it is not the doctor's responsibility to raise up and train that new baby? It is the responsibility of its father to see to its growth and development. Isn't that right?

In the same way, it's not yours or my responsibility to raise up and train the new births in God's kingdom. It's His job. After all, He is their Father, not me. And what's more, He's very capable of getting the job done. But this understanding doesn't satisfy the critics. In talking with them, you get the clear impression that they have more faith in the Devil than they do in God. They don't trust God to raise up His own children.

When I teach in other churches about follow-up, I always make it a point to ask for a show of hands of how many people received follow-up after they got saved. Most of the time, there are only a few hands raised. The vast majority of people tell me they had absolutely no follow-up, yet here they are in a class learning how to lead others to Christ.

Saints of God, you are not personally responsible to train up every person who prays with you to receive Jesus. God is very capable of raising up and training His own children. God will bring along others to minister to them. You're not solely responsible for their Christian development."

I don't want to give the impression that we don't do anything about follow-up because we do. When I first went out, the only thing I had to give out was tracts. Later, when I headed up the evangelism ministry, we were able to hand out more literature. In addition to the tract, we give them mini-books to read, and a brochure telling them about our church. Inside the brochure is a list of recommended churches in the entire Twin City area. We encourage them to attend one of them on a regular basis. If they don't have a Bible, we give them one. We tell them about our downtown mission and our television broadcast. We make known to them many different places in which they can get ministry. It's up to them to get there.

The subject of follow up is of special importance to me, because I've seen it has been a major roadblock preventing churches from going out street witnessing. It makes me shudder when I think how the Devil has sabotaged many a soul-winning plans because of that kind of reasoning. Many pastors have told me that they were, indeed, holding their congregation back from street witnessing simply because of the follow-up question. But after I shared with them my own experience, they changed their thinking and now have regularly scheduled evangelistic outings and are experiencing great success.

As valuable as Bibles, literature and church lists are, the most important thing we do for our new converts is pray for them. As a ministry team, we lift them up in prayer, pleading the blood of Jesus over their lives.

False Salvations

Now let's talk about the matter of those so-called "false salvations." There have been people that we prayed with and a few weeks later, we'd meet them and there was very little evidence that their lives had changed. People started saying that these were false salvations. They argue, "Since their life hasn't changed, they didn't really get saved. It's not enough just to say a simple prayer. They need to confess all their sins and repent of them. And the evidence of true repentance is a completely changed lifestyle with no smoking, alcohol, drugs, gambling, gangs and everything else."

They ask me, "How can people continue to live in sin if they truly have accepted Christ?" I ask them, "Well, how do you do it?" They look at me shocked and indignant and say, "Hey, I don't drink or do drugs." I simply respond, "Maybe not but have you ever sinned since you were saved?" Right away, I remind them of I John 1:8 before they answer. Then I ask, "How can you continue to sin if you are truly saved?"

The point I'm trying to make is that we should never judge the salvation of others. I know from the Word of God (and from 23 years of personal experience) that praying a simple prayer, asking Jesus to be Lord and Savior is all it takes to get someone saved. Romans 10:9-10 says, "That if thou shalt confess with thy mouth the Lord Jesus, and shalt believe in thine heart that God hath raised him from the dead, thou shalt be saved. For with the heart man believeth unto righteousness; and with the mouth confession is made unto salvation."

Did you catch that? It says if you confess with your mouth and believe in your heart that you "shall" get saved – not "might" get saved. Furthermore, verse 13 says, "whosoever shall call on the name of the Lord shall be saved." When I got saved, that's all I did. I asked Jesus to come into my life and then I told the first person I saw about it. I didn't make a list of every sin I ever committed and begged God to forgive me for them. There was no sobbing my guts out in "true" repentance. No. All I did was believe in my heart and confess with my mouth and I got saved.

Man Looks on the Outward Appearance

The reason why so many are prone to judging the salvation of others is because man judges by the outward appearance. But thankfully, God is able to see our hearts and He judges us from what He finds there. The Word of God tells us in no uncertain terms that we are not to judge. It says in Romans 14:4, "Who art thou that judgest another man's servant? to his own master he standeth or falleth. Yea, he shall be holden up: for God is able to make him stand…"

If the Christians in the church of Corinth were held up to this kind of judgment, I'm afraid all of them would be labeled as false salvations because they were so carnal that Paul said that even unbelievers didn't do the things they were doing. Paul said to them in, 1 Cororinthians 3:1, "And I, brethren, could not speak unto you as unto spiritual, but as unto carnal, even as unto babes in Christ." Paul called them "babes in Christ." That's an important thing to remember about people who have just experienced the new birth. They are babies. You shouldn't expect baby Christians to act like mature adults immediately. We need to give them time to grow up. That growth process is slower in some than it is in others.

We know that we are not saved by works (Eph. 2:8-9), so why do we want someone's salvation to be gauged by their works? We see this truth in nature as well. Tree saplings do not bear fruit right away. They need time to develop and mature before they begin bearing fruit. Just because they do not bear fruit, doesn't mean they are not alive. It's the same way with the young or baby Christians. They need time to grow up and mature in God.

The Conditions for Growth

The Word shows us that it is possible for someone to be genuinely saved, go to heaven, and never experience the fullness of God while on this earth. It says in 1 Timothy 2:4, "Who will have all men to be saved, and to come unto the knowledge of the truth." Getting saved comes first, then after that comes the knowledge of the truth. It is possible to experience salvation and not experience the knowledge of the fullness of truth.

Also, look what it says in Acts 26:18, "To open their eyes, and to turn them from darkness to light, and from the power of Satan unto God, that they may receive forgiveness of sins, and inheritance among them which are sanctified by faith that is in me." You receive the forgiveness of sins (that's salvation) "and" an inheritance. Inheritance is the fullness of God. Every believer will receive their inheritance in heaven but because of a lack of knowledge or failure to grow and mature in God, many Christians may not experience their inheritance on earth.

The simple truth is that growing and developing in the fullness of God is a process. It takes time. Some Christians grow faster than others. Though the prayer they prayed to receive Jesus might have been genuine, it is still up to them to choose life and blessing. Deuteronomy 30:19 tells us to choose life and blessing or death and cursing. If the new believer doesn't read the Bible, doesn't begin attending church, but rather chooses to keep company with the world, they themselves choose to live under the curse, never appropriating the inheritance of the saints of God. It's up to each of us to choose.

When someone prays the prayer of salvation, something supernatural takes place inside them. New life begins. They become a new creature in Christ. As evangelists, we tell them to find a good church and to attend it faithfully. We give them a Bible and urge them to read it and pray every day. But we cannot make them go to church. We can't make them read the Bible. And we can't make them pray every day. We have to trust that God, their father, will complete that work He started in their hearts.

Sometimes we fret and worry too much about people when God is at work in their lives right from the start. I remember a testimony that Carrie and Jody told me about a man named Carl. They met Carl at Catholic Charities and shared Jesus with him. Right away, he was eager to pray to receive Jesus. Afterward, Carl asked them about our church's drug treatment program. They encouraged him to call the church the next day to get more information on it. The girls prayed with Carl for deliverance from alcohol and to receive admittance to the treatment program. But Carl never did make that call. The girls simply stood in agreement over Carl and prayed for God's help and direction on his life. They trusted God to complete the work in Carl.

About six weeks later, they ran into Carl again. He explained he didn't call our church's treatment facility because he found one closer to him and went through the program. He said, "I've been drug and alcohol free ever since you prayed with me." He went on to say that he's gone to church every week and even started bringing his children with him and that God was restoring and healing his relationship with them. To God be the glory! God knows how to take care of His children. The apostle Paul said, "for I know whom I have believed and am persuaded that he is able to keep that which I have committed unto him..."(2 Timothy1:12)

When we pray with someone to receive Jesus, we must learn to trust God that he will complete the work in them. The Word says God is able to keep those that we pray with from falling and to present them faultless before the presence of His glory with exceeding joy. (Jude 24)

God Does His Own Follow-up

It's been 23 years since I've been street witnessing. I've prayed with literally thousands of people to get saved and I've never done follow-up on any of them besides giving them the handouts we give to all new converts. I've met many of these people after I prayed with them and I've been privileged to see the fruit of God working in their lives. There are far too many to share, but I'll give you a few of my favorite testimonies.

Just recently, I was in White Castle one night when I saw a man sitting at a table looking positively depressed. I asked him, "Can I sit down?" He asked me to join him and I proceeded to share Jesus with him and he prayed with me. He lit up like a Christmas tree. Several weeks later, I met him walking down the street. He looked so different, I barely recognized him. He told me how happy he was, and that he's been to church every week since.

I remember another life-changing account with a man named Stanley. I first saw him leaning up against a building, looking very disheveled. I approached him and asked, "Do you want to hear some good news?" He said "yes" so I told him about Jesus and right away he prayed with me. At the time, he was addicted to cocaine and he lost everything in his life that was important. He lost his job. His wife left him, taking with her their twin daughters. He lost all his possessions and was living on the street. I ministered to him for awhile about how God wants us to have an abundant life. He thanked me and I went on my way.

Three years later, I saw Stanley again, this time looking quite different. I was walking down the sidewalk when I heard someone yelling my name. I turned to see a man in a car, parking at the side of the street. He said, "Pastor Nick, do you remember me? Three years ago you prayed with me." I thought for a moment and then I remembered his name. I said, "Sure I do. You're Stanley, right?"

"Yes, and I'm doing a lot better than the last time you saw me." Was he ever! It was a night and day difference. He was smartly dressed in a business suit, sitting in a new Cadillac with his two daughters in the backseat. He said, "I want you to know that ever since you prayed with me that day, I have never touched drugs again. I got my life back. I have a good job, my wife came back and these are my two daughters."

God restored his life completely. In the three years after I prayed with him, God worked mightily in his life in spite of my not giving Stanley any follow up. Do you see how God is a capable Father, well able to take care and watch over His children?

Two workers, Ruth and Mark shared this testimony with me. They were waiting at their pick-up point waiting for the bus to pick them up to go back to church. They saw a drunken young man named Michael on the corner with some friends. He was in a really good mood, singing and dancing, and acting goofy. He was talking to everybody, even the evangelists. Ruth asked him if he was born again; he said he was but that alcohol was a real problem in his life and he needed help. Michael asked them to pray for him. They laid hands on him and Ruth asked God to deliver him from alcohol and set him on the right path for his life. They said his whole countenance changed and they could sense the power of God on him. The bus came and they parted ways.

Two months later, Mark saw Michael get off a bus one day. He said, "I recognized him right away. I said to him, 'Michael, how are you doing, brother?' He didn't know who in the world I was. I reminded him of the time we talked and prayed with him. He remembered and then, like a flood, he excitedly told me how much his life had changed. He had a good job, was attending a Bible-believing church and was free of alcohol."

He went on to tell Mark that since that night when they prayed for him, God had sent many people into his life to encourage him, build him up, and bless him in ways he never knew possible.

That's how God raises up His children – through a combined effort using all the members in the body of Christ.

Chapter Seven

Without a Vision, the People Perish

One of the most important things I learned from my pastor is the importance of getting a vision, or plan, from God about your life and ministry. He considers it so important that he preaches about it at the beginning of every new year. He says not only does God have a plan of redemption for all of mankind, but He has a specific plan for every person as well. And God also has a specific plan for every ministry.

Hab. 2:2 says, "...write the vision, and make it plain upon tables, that he may run that readeth it."

About our church's vision, Pastor tells us, "I have an obligation to share with you on a regular basis the vision God gave this ministry. As the one who has been charged with the responsibility for this corporate vision, I have to make the vision plain to you, to communicate it in a way that will give you momentum and direction to the effort you make toward the overall vision for this church."

He explains that some people don't have a clue as to what God's vision is for their life. They're just living each day as it comes, aimlessly and without purpose. Then there are other people who do have a vision for their life, only the vision isn't God-ordained. It's their own plan that came out of their own fleshly desires. God wants us to run with *His* vision – not ours. God doesn't want us to be in the dark about His plan. He doesn't want us wondering why we are here on this earth. God wants you to know what His vision is for your life so you can run with it.

He says without vision, you will never experience your full potential in God. You've got to get the vision down firmly in your heart before you can run with it. Without a vision, you won't have any direction or momentum for what you're doing. Once you get God's vision and you start making steps toward that vision, God will begin to supernaturally order your steps to take you toward that divinely appointed destiny.

Not only is there is an overall vision for our church, but our pastor expects each person in charge of any ministerial area in the church to get God's vision for that particular area of ministry. Every year, he meets with each head of ministry and goes over the vision. When I came on staff as the evangelism pastor, he expected me to get God's vision for evangelism as well.

Having a vision for ministry is more important than most people realize. Amos 3:3 asks, "Can two walk together except they be agreed?" How can any group of people work together effectively, striving toward a goal if they don't even know what their goal is? Without a common focus, no ministry will ever attain the best God has for it. In fact, vision is so important that Proverbs 29:18 warns us, "Where there is no vision, the people perish."

The most powerful demonstration of united vision is in Genesis 11:6. Nimrod, a godless and rebellious man, was leading the people in a rebellion against God. They were in the process of building the infamous Tower of Babel, a tower so tall it would reach the heavens, providing them an escape from the wrath of God in case He ever decided to flood the earth again. About their unity in purpose God said this:

> *And the Lord said, Behold, the people is one, and they have all one language; and this they begin to do: and now nothing will be restrained from them, which they have imagined to do.* (Genesis 11:6)

For any group of people that is united in vision and purpose, who speak the same thing, the Bible says, "nothing will be restrained from them." *That* is the power of corporate vision.

About agreement Jesus said, "…if two of you shall agree on earth as touching any thing that they shall ask, it shall be done for them of my Father which is in heaven." (Matt 18:19) If any two people agree together, God will grant their petition. An excellent petition we can all agree together for the fulfillment of is in Psalms 2:8:

> *Ask of me, and I shall give thee the heathen for thine inheritance, and the uttermost parts of the earth for thy possession.*

God wants us to ask Him for souls. He says if we ask, He'll give them to us. So let's start asking.

Setting Your Vision

We have asked God for all the unsaved in the Minneapolis-St. Paul area. In fact, the core vision for the Evangelism Ministry of Living Word Christian Center is to win the people in the Twin Cities for the Lord Jesus Christ and then to expand that to include reaching those throughout the world.

With that being our overall vision, we break that vision down into yearly goals. In the beginning years, my pastor and I would pray together to get from God what he calls a "soul goal" – the number of salvations we believe God for in one year's time. The first year we set a soul goal was in 1986. The pastor and I prayed together and God gave each of us the same number of 1500 souls. Every year that goal has increased in size as our faith to believe Him for more souls increases.

One evening when Pete and I were downtown Minneapolis, he turned to me and by the Spirit said, "One day, Nick, you will have to use school buses to carry all the laborers out into the harvest field." Praise God, it was only two months later when that came to pass! Today, twenty years later, there have been many evenings when we have had 200 (one time we had as many as 400) laborers on the streets and we pray with 1500-2000 people in one evening. To God be all the glory!

Just as the pastor shares the overall vision for the church with the congregation on a regular basis, I too share the vision for the Evangelism Ministry with those in my ministry. I share it so we all have something we can agree on and attach our faith to and believe God for.

In addition to the overall vision of the ministry, we have goals for the number of people we pray with in one evening and for the number of laborers that come out with us street witnessing. We also have a vision for our missions, prison and nursing home outreaches as well. Every time we go out to share the Gospel, we set a corporate goal for that night and each team leader sets a goal for his or her team as well.

Before we hit the streets, we pray together in faith and ask God for the heathen and use our faith to obtain the goals He has set before us. Ninety-five percent of the time, we make that goal. Many times, we go well over the goal and there are evenings when we don't make the goal. And if we don't, so what? The Bible says the angels in heaven rejoice over one sinner that comes to repentance. If we take a bus load of laborers somewhere and only pray with one person to get saved, our effort was not in vain. Praise God, that one person is saved out of spending an eternity in hell.

Each time we press toward a vision or goal and we make it, our faith is built up and we are able to believe God for greater increase. I believe that, that is how God wants us to use our faith.

Counting People

Any time you set a goal, you need to keep track of your progress toward meeting that goal. How else would you know whether or not you make the goal? If you're believing God for a certain number of people to get saved, then that means you will be counting the number of people that you pray with. Oddly enough, the aspect of counting people bothers some believers. They think it's somehow unspiritual. I tell them, "We count people because people count."

It's perfectly scriptural to keep count of people. The Bible says angels rejoice over one sinner that repents. And in the book of Acts it says on the day of Pentecost there were 120 people in the upper room. How did they know there were exactly 120 people in the upper room unless someone took the time to count them? And on that same day, the Bible says that after Peter got done preaching to the multitudes that 3000 people got saved that day. Brothers and sisters, somebody took the time to count those people. Does anybody read that account in the Bible and think "How unspiritual! They counted the people." No! We're all amazed by the numbers.

I tell people evangelism is a mathematical equation.

"God *adds* to the Church daily such as should be saved."

"At the same time, He *subtracts* from Satan's kingdom."

"As the saints go forth, we *multiply* in disciples."

"Jesus *divides* the portion of the goods between those who are saved."

That, my friends, is divine math. I'm only teasing, but you get my point. Don't get hung up about numbers. There is nothing unspiritual – and certainly not unscriptural – about counting the number of people you pray with to receive Jesus.

However, I will say that while keeping track of progress toward a specific goal provides motivation for the group to strive for, there is a trap that you must watch out for and that is a "numbers-only" game. Sometimes people lose their focus. You have to remind them that the goal is not the number itself, but rather the souls rescued out of Satan's kingdom that, that number represents.

One way I discourage the "numbers-only" mentality is that I don't allow the teams to openly share the number of people they prayed with in an evening. I used to hear comments like, "How many did you get? We got 20 tonight!" To eliminate that behavior, I have the team leaders write down their total for the night and give it to the bus captain when he picks us up, and then I share the overall number the entire team prayed with when we get back to the church. This keeps a spirit of competition out of the ministry effort. And it also protects some workers from becoming discouraged and closes the door on boasting for others.

Your Own Personal Vision

Some have asked me, "How do I get a vision for my life personally?" The answer is simple. You get it through prayer, by spending time in the presence of God. The Bible says in Psalms 37:4-5, "Delight thyself also in the Lord; and he shall give thee the desires of thine heart. Commit thy way unto the Lord; trust also in him; and he shall bring it to pass."

You get a vision for your life by asking God to give you a vision. The Bible says He'll give you the desires of your heart. God first implants desires within your heart and then He works to fulfill those desires.

Once He's given you a vision, be careful not to look to your own natural abilities to fulfill it. Trust God to direct you and to bring it to pass. As you start taking steps in that direction, He'll begin to guide and direct you supernaturally.

Don't despise small beginnings. The size of your vision doesn't matter. What matters is that you have one. Start where you are right now. For some, it would be a stretch of faith just to go out on the streets and support the team with prayer. If that's where you are, then go with that. When you've overcome that fear, perhaps the next thing you can believe God for is to go out once a month with a goal of praying with 10 people in that year. That's great! Don't ever think your supply is insignificant. You never know, one of those 10 people you prayed with might be the next Billy Graham. Don't allow yourself to be overwhelmed by the need of the world. God sees the big picture and He knows the whole plan. You'll do all right if you simply follow His leading for your life.

I encourage people to write down their personal visions and post them somewhere so they can see them every day, like on the refrigerator. Put up pictures and names of those you are believing God for their salvation. Every time you see their faces and their names, claim them for the kingdom of God. Ask the Lord of the harvest to send laborers across their paths to plant and water God's incorruptible seed.

Each time you go out, use your faith and expect people to pray with you. See yourself praying with and ministering to multitudes. I promise you, once you pray with a few people and realize how easy it is (because the anointing of God is doing all the work), you'll find your faith will increase and you'll expand your vision to believe God for more souls. Keep your vision before your spiritual eyes and in your mouth and you'll be amazed at what the Lord will do through you.

Chapter Eight

The How-To's
of Evangelism

Whenever I minister in other churches about evangelism, the most requested information people want to hear about is what I call the "how to's." I'm more than willing to share about this topic, but I try to be careful not to come across as though I think this is the only way you should operate an evangelistic ministry. On the contrary, I know that God has a specific plan and vision for every ministry and we need to follow His plan. Yet I know that I've benefited from hearing about the "nuts and bolts" of how other similar ministries function. So with that understanding, I will share how we operate our evangelism ministry.

A Typical Evangelistic Outing

I'll start by giving you the step-by-step rundown of a typical evangelism outing. First of all, we all meet together at church one hour before we actually get on the buses and go out to the streets. I begin with prayer and then teach for about 45 minutes or as the Spirit of God leads. I exhort everyone from the Word on the subject of evangelism, share a few testimonies, and then give a few examples of how to minister to people on the street. Even though most of the people there have heard it dozens of times, my teaching is specifically geared toward people who are new at going out on the streets.

I have found that this time of prayer and teaching is vital to the success of the outing. Most of our outings are in the evening and the people going out have just gotten off from their nine-to-five jobs. Their minds are full of the day's activities. Many times their day was full of difficulties and unpleasant things. They come to evangelism with the weight of all these worldly things on their mind. The prayer and teaching helps them to release their stress and cares onto the Lord and to focus their minds on God. In fact, many people "drag" themselves to church, not really feeling in the "mood' to minister. But after prayer and teaching, their hearts are revived and they are able to hit the streets full of love, full of joy, and full of God.

Another interesting ministry aspect of this time of teaching is that God often uses it to prepare us for what is ahead that night. Many times, without my knowing it, I'll begin to speak prophetically about what may happen that night. When the evening is over, someone will come up to me and say, "Pastor Nick, what you said tonight in the teaching actually happened to me."

For instance, one time while I was teaching I said the words, "What happens when we pray with people is that they decide not to kill themselves, they decide not to jump off that bridge." That night, one of my workers came up to me very excited. They said, "Nick, what you said about the person not jumping off the bridge… that happened tonight." They approached a very dejected-looking young man. When they shared Jesus with him, he was eager to pray. God moved on Him wonderfully. There was an immediate change to his expression and demeanor. Afterward he shocked them by saying, "Before you prayed with me, I had just made the decision to kill myself by jumping off a bridge." We all praised God for that divine intervention. Glory to God!

Another time I said simply, "We might be walking along and see someone sitting on the street corner drinking a Colt 45. They need Jesus." Again, one of our teams was walking along the street and saw someone sitting on the corner. They felt prompted by the Spirit of God to talk to him. He too eagerly prayed to receive Jesus. As they walked away, one of them realized that he was sitting on the street drinking a Colt 45, just as I had unknowingly prophesied.

One night I had two pages of notes that I was going to teach on before going out on the streets. As I began teaching, the Lord changed the direction of my message. I felt compelled to talk about a particular crime that happened a few nights before on Hennepin Avenue in downtown Minneapolis. A young man was attacked and beaten to death by three other young men in broad daylight. No one came to this young man's aid and the young men were still at large. The anointing of God manifested itself in me in the form of righteous indignation about the Devil's blatant contamination of our city. I hated what the Devil had done. So strong were my feelings that we lifted it up to the Lord in prayer before we went out.

You can imagine my surprise when my team and I were walking down Hennepin Avenue and came face to face with 17 members of this young man's family. They were at the very site where the murder had taken place and were placing roses on the spot where he died. Praise God, what supernatural timing! I approached the parents and introduced myself and explained that I was a pastor from a church here in the cities. I told them, "I was sorry to hear about your son. But I want you to know something; God didn't take your son's life. It was the work of the Devil. The Bible says he comes to steal, kill, and to destroy. God comes to give life and to give it more abundantly." They readily received what I had to say and every one of them prayed to receive Jesus. Glory to God!

What's more, I asked them if they wanted prayer for anything and they said, "We would like our son's killers to be caught so they don't kill someone else's son." We held hands and prayed that the three youth would be overwhelmed by the guilt of their crime and turn themselves in to the authorities. That's exactly what happened. They turned themselves in the next day. Isn't God good?

Assigning Teams

I have everyone sign in when they arrive. While I'm teaching, a couple of my leaders will group everyone into ministry teams of three. (Again, it is remarkable how the Holy Spirit will guide the assembly of each team to meet that night's specific ministry needs.) They designate one person to be the leader for each group. The leader is the one who approaches people on the street and does the majority of ministering. The other two are there to support the leader by praying for him throughout the evening, to carry follow-up literature and, most of all, to protect the anointing of God. I should make this point about praying. The helpers are there to pray in the Spirit, but they're to do it under their breath so no one can see or hear them. Praying out loud would not only be distracting, but weird-looking as well.

In case you might be tempted to think the helpers' jobs are not as important, let me set you straight. If the helpers weren't there protecting and guarding the anointing, I can guarantee you, very little fruit would be accomplished for the night. The Devil will do anything to bust up the conversation the leader is having with an unsaved person. When they are deep in conversation, a passerby will make a beeline toward them and interrupt to ask an unimportant question like, "What time is it?" or "Do you have a dollar?" These people are sent directly from Satan to disrupt the flow of ministry and to destroy the anointing. And it happens frequently. It is the helpers' job to intersect all such interruptions. They simply approach them and start witnessing to them. They either get saved or leave.

Depending on the experience of the two helpers, the leader does most of the talking. We do, however, encourage everyone to step out and minister at some point. We want newcomers to mostly just pray and observe their first time out. Their time should be spent observing and listening to the leader to learn how we function together as a team. When they're comfortable, we let them minister. For some, that's almost immediate. For others, it might take them a much longer time before they feel comfortable enough to approach someone. We're careful not to push anyone to minister until they're ready. We let them progress in their own time.

When I'm done teaching, we all gather together in a circle and pray, standing on the scripture in Psalms 2:8, "Ask of me, and I shall give thee the heathen for thine inheritance." We assemble the teams together and then head out to the bus.

We have learned the wisdom in asking God in what area He wants us to minister in. It makes a world of difference. In the beginning, we sent our evangelism teams into the neighborhoods that were near our church. But the fruit was pitiful. When we sought God about it, He told us to go to a different part of the city. We obeyed and started to have great success. You, too, need to ask God to show you what part of the city to minister in. He knows where the people are hungry and ready to receive.

While on the bus, the leader of each team goes over their individual vision they have for the night and pray together as a team. Typically, we pray for protection, direction, and the utterance of God.

Our bus captain drops the teams off at two or more designated points in the city. After an hour to an hour and a half, he comes back at the same place to pick everyone up to go back to the church. When we get back, I announce the total number of people who prayed to receive Jesus. (I remind everyone that the success of each team's effort is not measured by how many people they led to the Lord, but rather their success is measured by how they stayed together in unity and followed the leading of the Holy Spirit.) We give everyone an opportunity to share testimonies of what happened that night. The night's outing is closed by praying for the people who got saved that night.

Protect the Anointing

If you want to experience any fruit at all, do everything possible to protect the anointing of God that is on your teams. I don't care how bold you are, without the anointing of God operating in your ministry, you'll waste your time. If you want to flow in the corporate anointing, you will have to take steps to protect it because the Devil will do everything he can to rob it from you. He knows that without the burden removing, yoke destroying power of God, you are little threat to the kingdom of darkness.

First of all, keep strife out. James 3:16 says, "For where envying and strife is, there is confusion and every evil work." If Satan can breed division within your ranks, he can destroy your effectiveness as a ministry. Instill in your workers the understanding that strife opens the door to destruction. I constantly remind my workers about the danger of strife, envy and jealousy. I tell them it doesn't belong here. But we're all human and sometimes those feelings will crop up. Someone might feel slighted because they weren't assigned to be the leader of their team. Or they might not be happy with whom they've been teamed up with, not liking the leader's witnessing "style." I tell them to deal with it immediately and submit to their assigned authority. Protecting the anointing on the ministry is more important than these minor fleshy squabbles.

That's another reason I teach before we go out. It helps to stir up unity and one accord in our hearts. I tell them if we stay in unity and love, the same anointing that is on me, will flow to them "if" we stay in one accord. Consequently, that takes a joint effort from each one of us to guard our hearts. Never allow unforgiveness, selfishness, grumbling, or complaining to get a foot in the door. Keep it out. If you don't, the Devil will have ground to disrupt your effectiveness as a group.

I tell everyone to ask themselves the question, "What is my motive for going out on the streets?" Are you going so that people will notice you and think you're special? That you're more spiritual than the average Christian? That you're some kind of spiritual superstar? Have you ever found yourself boasting about how many people you prayed with?

These are all attitudes of pride. And the Bible says that God resists the proud. And that, my friend, is not a desirable place to be. Pride, sometimes, is difficult to recognize in ourselves. We need to examine our hearts on a continual basis.

The Four "P's" of Evangelism

Years ago, the Lord gave me a "formula" (if I may refer to it as that) for a successful night on the streets. The formula He gave me was doing four "P's" each time we go out. They are 1) Pray, 2) Praise, 3) Putting on the whole armor of God, and 4) Possessing the land.

Prayer

Let's first talk about prayer. Prayer must be at the foundation of every ministry. Too many Christians are trying to go out and do the work of the Lord without the covering of prayer. Talk about setting yourself up for failure! They're an accident waiting to happen. You must pray for God's direction, pray for His anointing, pray for protection, pray to be led of His Spirit, pray for boldness, pray for more laborers… and we are to pray for the salvation of souls.

Let me tell you the reason why our teams have so much success when they go out. It's because my pastor's wife and many others from church got together and prayed for the evangelism ministry every week. They wept and groaned in prayer birthing this ministry.

The Bible says in Eph 6:12, "For we wrestle not against flesh and blood, but against principalities, against powers, against the rulers of the darkness of this world, against spiritual wickedness in high places." In prayer, they took authority over the principalities and powers that were over the Twin City area. When we first started going out, it was tough getting anyone to pray with us. But now it's common for us to pray with hundreds of people every time we go out.

I want to show you something else about prayer. Look what it says in Hosea 10:12, "Sow to yourselves in righteousness, reap in mercy; <u>break up your fallow ground</u>: for it is time to seek the Lord, till he come and rain righteousness upon you."

We are to break up fallow ground. Fallow ground is soil that has been left standing season after season without anything being planted in it. The topsoil becomes so hard that when it rains, the water doesn't even soak into the ground. It simply sits on top of the soil. Trying to plant seeds in fallow ground would be impossible. There would be no fruit.

Fallow ground must first be prepared before you can plant seeds in it. How do you prepare fallow ground? By plowing it. The first time a farmer goes over the rocky soil with his plow, he'll have a field full of dirt clods. It's still not yet prepared to have seed planted in it. The farmer has to plow the field over and over until it is a finely combed field, with all the dirt clods having been broken down. When that happens, the field is ready to receive seed. The end result is that he'll have a bumper crop.

In the spirit realm, prayer has the same effect as the farmer plowing his fields. When people pray, they are preparing a mission field for the seed to be planted. Without the preparatory work of prayer, the teams would go out into the streets and sow God's incorruptible seed onto fallow ground. Consequently, there would be little fruit. I can't tell you how thankful I am for the people who stayed behind on Monday nights and prayed for us when we went out on the streets. Praise God! We all have a job to do. And it's important everyone does his or her part.

Praise

The second "P" in the formula of a successful night out on the streets is "praise." The Bible says in Psalms 22:3, "But thou art holy, O thou that inhabitest the praises of Israel." God inhabits the praises of His people. I tell my workers that if they have a night where they don't "feel" like going out on the streets because of depression or because they're full of fear, I tell them to begin praising God. When you praise Him, His strength comes every time. In fact, it is a spiritual law: praise brings the power of God on the scene. It's like plugging into a socket for electricity.

There are many biblical examples of this spiritual law, but one that immediately comes to mind is in Acts 16. Paul and Silas were in prison for preaching the Gospel. It says at midnight they began to praise God. There came an earthquake and all the prison doors flew open. Glory to God. Praise brought the power of God.

Another example is in 2 Chron 5:13-6:1, "It came even to pass, as the trumpeters and singers were as one, to make one sound to be heard in praising and thanking the Lord; and when they lifted up their voice with the trumpets and cymbals and instruments of musick, and praised the Lord, saying, For he is good; for his mercy endureth for ever: that then the house was filled with a cloud, even the house of the Lord; So that the priests could not stand to minister by reason of the cloud: for the glory of the Lord had filled the house of God."

The temple had just been completed and King Solomon had it dedicated to the Lord. In the scripture above, we see that when they began to praise God, His presence came. The glory of God came in like a cloud and it was so strong that the priests couldn't stand. They fell out under the power of God. Again, praise brought the power of God.

Now I want you to look at a scripture in Psalms 8:2, "Out of the mouth of babes and sucklings hast thou ordained strength because of thine enemies, that thou mightest still the enemy and the avenger." Praise stills the enemy. When the enemy is attacking, just start praising God and he will flee. As an example, I can give you a real-life testimony.

One night when I was on the streets witnessing, there was a man who began to verbally persecute me for witnessing. Wherever I went he followed, spewing out all kinds of garbage. Basically just mocking me. After a short while, I had had enough. I stopped, lifted my hands toward heaven and began to praise the Lord. Let me tell you, he couldn't get out of there fast enough.

Having a continual heart of praise is vital to your success on the streets.

Put on the Whole Armor of God

Now let's move on to the third "P" which is "putting on the armor of God." It says in Ephesians 6:13-17, "Wherefore take unto you the whole armour of God, that ye may be able to withstand in the evil day, and having done all, to stand. Stand therefore, having your loins girt about with truth, and having on the breastplate of righteousness; And your feet shod with the preparation of the gospel of peace; Above all, taking the shield of faith, wherewith ye shall be able to quench all the fiery darts of the wicked. And take the helmet of salvation, and the sword of the Spirit, which is the word of God."

Jesus died on the cross to provide us with this armor. We need to wear it every day because we're not wrestling with flesh and blood, we're wrestling with the god of this world (Satan). We should go forth full of the Word of God, walking in integrity. Keeping in mind that our purpose is to share the gospel of peace. Holding our shield of faith up high, we stand against Satan's lies of deceit, not letting him talk us out of the promises of God. And, lastly, we must skillfully use the sword of the Spirit which is the Word of God. The sword of the Spirit is unique from all the other armor in that it is the only piece that is used for offense, while all the other pieces are used for defense. We use the Word of God against the Devil – not against people. We are commanded to serve others in love. Never use the Word of God to condemn someone.

Having a full set of armor on, you can go out with confidence and in the authority of Jesus. The armor of God – never leave home without it.

Possess the Land

The last "P" in the formula for a successful night out witnessing is "possess the land." It says in Joshua 1:3, "Every place that the sole of your foot shall tread upon, that have I given unto you..."

After the foundation of prayer has been laid, it is now the responsibility of the laborers to physically go into the land and possess it. As I have shared before, when I first started going into the streets of downtown Minneapolis no one would pray with me. But we kept praying and going, and today when we go into that same area, literally hundreds will pray with us. We take from Satan's kingdom and possess the land.

You don't go into an area one time and think you've taken possession of it. Possessing the land happens through a process of time. After all, the children of Israel didn't possess all of the promised land the first day they crossed the river Jordan. It happened through a process of time. They literally had to run out the inhabitants from the land. That's what we do to Satan – run him out.

But rest assured, Satan will not leave without a struggle. He'll throw some persecution your way, but just remember he's already a defeated foe. God has already given you the land. We just have to go in and possess it.

Let me give you an example of possessing the land. One night a couple of years ago, I was in downtown Minneapolis witnessing outside a charitable organization called Catholic Charities. It's a wonderful charity that does a lot of work with the homeless. I thought it would be a great opportunity to be able to minister to the people inside. So I went in, introduced myself and asked them if I could minister to the people there. They told me no, but that I was welcome to stay outside and witness as they came out. I thanked them, and continued to minister to people on the outside every week.

As time went by, the workers at the charity got to know us and we won their trust, and eventually they invited us in to minister to those inside. Glory to God! Every Monday and Tuesday, we go to Catholic Charities and minister to the people there. We have prayed with literally hundreds of people, and have witnessed many wonderful miracles in the lives of the people there. That's only one example of possessing the land.

Crime Prevention

There is another interesting aspect about possessing the land. While in the act of sharing the Good News, we have unknowingly been instrumental in preventing various crimes from going down. In this way, we push back the kingdom of darkness by preventing Satan from manifesting his mayhem.

For instance, one of my workers, Ronnie, told me they prayed with a man who looked very angry. When he prayed the salvation prayer, true joy washed over this man. He then shocked Ronnie by saying that before they stopped to talk with him, he was on his way to kill someone.

That almost exact scenario happened to me as well. I saw a man walking across the street and I approached him. He seemed very agitated, but he listened to everything I had to say and, in the end, decided to pray with me. There was a distinct change in him. Afterward, he showed me a gun he had in his pocket and said that he was going to use it to kill someone that night. But the anger was all gone so he decided to go home instead. Two people became born again and, at the same time, two murders were prevented. God is good, isn't He?

There was a time I stopped a woman in downtown Minneapolis and I led her to the Lord. She told me that before I stopped her, she was on her way to do some shoplifting at one of the major department stores. This was a way of life for her, but she was instantly convicted in her heart that she had to stop it. Praise God, the crime rate keeps getting lower.

I prayed with a man named Bill who works at Catholic Charities. He was distraught because his 14-year-old daughter, Marion, ran away from home and he hadn't heard from her in a very long time. He didn't know if she was dead or alive. I told him about the scripture in Matthew 18:19 that says, "…that if two of you shall agree on earth as touching any thing that they shall ask, it shall be done for them of my Father which is in heaven." We lifted up his daughter to the Lord, and we prayed and agreed together that she would come home. Two weeks later, I went to Catholic Charities and talked to Bill. He had a special surprise for me. He led me over to the receptionist area and introduced me to his daughter who was working behind the desk. Praise God! I talked with Marion about the Lord and she prayed with me. I'm confident she'll not run away again.

Often God has used us to minister to people who have been the victims of crime, to bring God's love and healing into their lives. For instance, we heard on the news about an arson who set a house on fire as an act of retribution, killing five children. One of our workers, Doug, met and talked with one of their cousins. Doug ministered to him about the love of God. As a result, the cousin and his girlfriend became born again. Said Doug, "I asked him if they had any other needs we could pray about, and he replied bitterly, 'Yeah, pray that those who set the fire would fry.' I talked to him about the importance of justice being served and consequences for wrong behavior, then I ministered to him about how forgiveness and bitterness prevents God from working in our lives. We all joined hands and put this root of bitterness under the blood. God visibly moved on their hearts."

Two workers named Carolyn and Becky shared with me about a divine appointment they had one night. They met and prayed with two young boys who were around 10 and 12 years old. They shared how their babysitter stole them from their mother when they were only preschool age. It took five years before authorities caught her and the boys were reunited with their mother. They had been home for two years and had traveled the country doing talk shows. The experience messed up all their lives and they were still having trouble adapting to the change. Carolyn and Becky were used of God to bring healing to their lives and to undo the works of Satan.

Roxanne, Tom, and John were excited about an experience they had one night while praying with a young man to get saved. After praying, he told Roxanne, "I feel funny." She said, "What do you mean?" He proceeded to explain that he had just spent $50 to get high right before they came. He said, "When you approached me, you were just a blur. Now I'm completely sober. I just wasted 50 bucks." The "funny" he felt turned out to be the anointing of God.

But that's a very common occurrence on the streets. Drunks and drug addicts sober up instantly when we pray for them. It always amazes them.

Another thing that happens frequently is the number of people that God has used us in preventing them from committing suicide. I'm always deeply grateful when that happens.

There are many more examples I could give, but it would take up too much space. Crime and crisis prevention is a wonderful product of our endeavor to possess the land. We thank God that He uses us in this fashion. It's all a part of doing the work of Jesus in the earth and taking back what the Devil has stolen.

Put on Humility

There is an understanding that is vital for all Christians to embrace if he is to be successful at soul winning. It's found in John 15:5, "I am the vine, ye are the branches: He that abideth in me, and I in him, the same bringeth forth much fruit: for without me ye can do nothing."

Jesus said, "without me, you can do nothing." Don't be offended by what I'm about to say, but you are not smart enough, educated enough, or clever enough to bring about any lasting change in another human being apart from God almighty. And I mean *nothing.* It's not you, but God in you and through you who brings about change in another person's life. For that reason, you cannot take credit for souls won to Jesus, for people being healed and delivered, or filled with the Holy Spirit. For you to take credit for these things is about as foolish as the computer I'm using to write this book to take credit for the finished work. Just like my computer, we are all tools in the hands of God, which He uses to bring about change in the lives of those around us.

This understanding is the foundation that is necessary for us to have which, in turn, enables us to embrace the truth in Philippians 4:13 which says, "I can do all things through Christ who strengthens me." Isn't that interesting? The knowledge that you can do nothing outside of Christ is the platform from which you can go forth and do all things "through" Christ. If we base our lives and ministry on the truth of His Word and if we follow the leading of the Holy Spirit, there is nothing you can't accomplish in Christ Jesus.

Having and embracing this truth will keep you from being seduced by spiritual pride. You can be used of God to do great things and stay humble when you constantly remind yourself that it's not you doing the work. It's God who is doing the work – you're just His tool.

Using Wisdom

The Bible says in Proverbs 11:30, "The fruit of the righteous is a tree of life; and he that winneth souls is wise."

He that wins souls is wise. I have found that the wisdom we've learned from twenty-three years of street witnessing makes our times on the streets go much more smoothly and without incident. There are several common-sense things I'd like to pass on to you that, I think, you'll appreciate knowing "before" you approach a stranger on the street.

While you're trying to get people saved, the Devil's group will try and interfere with your efforts any way they can. They'll attempt to bring fear, confusion, distrust, and anything else to prevent you from sharing the Gospel message. For that reason, it's important that we are sensitive to what an unbeliever's perception of us might be. Remember that you are a complete stranger to them. They don't know you or what your intention is. For that reason, we must strive to be as non-threatening as possible.

Take heed to the following advice. Always approach people within their field of view. Be aware of your tone of voice and the words you choose. Are you conveying genuine love and understanding? Also, make direct eye contact while you're talking and listen to them when they respond to you. Don't interrupt them or cut them off. In fact, listen for clues in what they say that will help you to know how to minister to them. Make sure you're dressed appropriately for the kind of people you expect to encounter. Who would want to listen to someone who looks worse off then they do?

And for heaven's sake, smile.

Don't Argue or Get in Strife

Paul wrote to the Colossians, "Walk in wisdom toward them that are without, redeeming the time. Let your speech be always with grace, seasoned with salt, that ye may know how ye ought to answer every man." (Colossians 4:5-6)

The phrase "redeeming the time" is another way of saying "make the most of every opportunity that comes." The Devil will try to waste and rob you of precious time on the streets by putting those in your path who will argue with you on some point of doctrine. These people, no matter how long you talk with them, never make a decision to pray. They're just wasting your time. You need to end the conversation and move on. Politely tell them that you don't want to argue and that Jesus loves them. The Bible says a soft answer turns away wrath. Always speak in tones of gentleness and humility. Sometimes this can be difficult because some of these people know how to push your buttons. Don't blow up, just walk away. This is the exact same advice the apostle Paul told Timothy in 2 Tim 2:23-24: "But foolish and unlearned questions avoid, knowing that they do gender strifes. And the servant of the Lord must not strive; but be gentle unto all men, apt to teach, patient."

One of my workers, Troy, shared with me his experience in being drawn into one of these contentious situations – a situation that was ineffective and downright ugly.

He said, "I approached some people and talked to them about the Lord. They didn't receive at all. In fact, they got downright mad at me. Unfortunately, I got in the flesh and tried to convince them on my own, using every tactic I could think of. They became all the more angry and started using filthy language, some of which I've never heard before. After they left, I was so grieved in my heart. I repented and asked God to forgive me. I learned my lesson and will never allow myself to get in the flesh like that again."

Please, please, please don't allow yourself to be drawn into arguments about doctrinal differences or traditions. Stay on common ground like Jesus' death, burial, and resurrection. Using common ground, lead them to Jesus and then as they begin to grow, the Holy Spirit will guide them into all truth. It's pointless to try to change someone's views or opinions about doctrine when they're not even born again. When dealing with the unsaved you need to deal with the "must" issues first and then after that, the "should" issues. (Everyone "should" live holy... but they "must" be born again.)

Sometimes they'll draw the conversation into some other direction by asking questions that have nothing to do with salvation. Don't be rude or abrupt with them, but as quickly as possible bring the conversation back to the topic of salvation. Some of them are asking questions out of sincerity. But others are just looking for an argument, looking for a chance to trip you up. Answer the sincere questions if you can. To the others looking for an argument, say something like this, "I don't know about that, but I do know that when I die, I'm going to heaven. Are you?"

Avoid Threatening Behavior

That brings me to another important point. Never start a conversation (especially with children) by saying, "If you were to die tonight..." Some people get freaked out about it. Trust me. This I know.

We try to eliminate all behavior that might appear threatening. Put yourself in their shoes. If a stranger approached you with his eyes locked on yours, then slipped his hand inside his coat, what might you think? It's not unreasonable for them to think you were reaching for a weapon. The world is full of sin and people are afraid. For that reason, when you walk up to someone, have ready in your hand a tract or whatever literature you're handing out, visible for them to see. This will eliminate any embarrassing scenes.

Study to Show Thyself Approved

If you want people to avoid you like the plague, tote around a great big Bible the size of a seat cushion. Big Bibles intimidate some people. Others, spotting your great big Bible, will figure out what you're up to and they'll go to great lengths to avoid you. We suggest you carry a small pocket Bible for those times when you need to use it. But generally, we try to rely on memorized scripture. (The Holy Spirit will remind you of whatever scripture you need, when you need it.)

I'd like to make a few comments along these lines. It's true you can win souls with having knowledge of only two scriptures, but you should learn more of the Word of God so God can use you in even greater ways. We are admonished in 2 Timothy 2:15, "Study to shew thyself approved unto God, a workman that needeth not to be ashamed, rightly dividing the word of truth."

As a minister of the Word of God (and we're all called to minister the Word), you should be growing in knowledge and understanding of the Word. This requires you to study the Word on a regular basis. Make it a habit to read and study the Bible every day. If you're serious about soul winning, this should be a priority for you.

I encourage those in my ministry to commit as much scripture to memory, so you aren't slowed down by having to look it up while you're in the middle of a conversation. The more Word you memorize, the more Word the Holy Spirit has to bring to your remembrance. Romans 10:8 says, "But what saith it? The word is nigh thee, even in thy mouth, and in thy heart: that is, the word of faith, which we preach." You have to put the Word of God in your heart before it can come out of your mouth.

Witnessing Near Stores

We have a lot of success near store fronts and larger store parking lots, but we've found it's best not to approach people when they're on their way into the store. Their minds are occupied with what they need to purchase or about the errand they need to get done. They'll most likely brush you off because they "don't have time" to listen. Some have gone as far as complain to the store manager about us, which resulted in us having to leave.

Instead, wait to talk to people on their way out of the store, away from the door. With their shopping completed, they're more likely to take the time and talk with you. If they don't receive, they'll just go on their way and not do anything to hinder your work.

Avoid the Appearance of Evil

It's important that we avoid the very appearance of evil. Avoid doing anything that anyone could bring an accusation against you to discredit you. And, believe me, there are those who would love the opportunity to discredit the Word of God and all believers any way they can. Don't do anything to help them. Maintain the highest level of integrity.

For instance, a man should never approach a woman unless he has another woman with him. And likewise, a woman should never approach a man alone. Be very cautious when talking with children. It's very scary for parents these days to have strangers walk up to their kids and talk to them. The Devil would love to plant perverted thoughts about you in an onlooker's mind. Only talk to kids out in the open in full view of anyone that could be watching. Do not hug or touch a child except for maybe a brief handshake.

Keep the salvation prayer with children simple. "Jesus, come into my heart. Be my friend. Be my Savior. Be my Lord. Thank you, Jesus." We've also found that adult tracts are not appropriate for children, so we use tracts designed just for children. As I mentioned briefly before, never talk to children about dying or going to heaven. You don't want them to think they're going to die or have to be separated from their family. Use common sense.

If their parents are present, talk to them first and get permission from them to talk to their children. It's interesting to see, but often a parent will not pray with us initially. But when they see their children praying, they end up praying along with them. Every time I see this, I thank God for His wisdom.

Wisdom for Backsliders

Occasionally, we run into someone who once knew the Lord but has fallen away from Him. They know the truth and often can quote you the scriptures you're sharing with them. The most important thing to remember about ministering to these people is to never condemn or judge them.

Galatians 6:1 tells us, "Brethren, if a man be overtaken in a fault, ye which are spiritual, restore such an one in the spirit of meekness; considering thyself, lest thou also be tempted."

They often tell me, "I'm a backslider." I tell them, "Just slide right back. You may have walked away from God, but He's never walked away from you. He hasn't left nor forsaken you. He's not mad at you for messing up. He still loves you and wants to fellowship with you. Don't run from God. Run back to Him. He's not given up on you."

If they decide to pray with me, I'll lead them in a prayer something like this. "Lord, I know that I'm backslid, but right now I want to slide back to You. You said in Your Word that if I confess my sins, You're faithful and just to forgive me of my sins and to cleanse me from all unrighteousness. Thank You, Jesus, for loving me and forgiving me, in the name of Jesus. Amen."

Nuggets of Wisdom

- When talking to people, acknowledge their personal boundaries by staying at least 18 inches apart from them.
- Remember to be prayed up before you go out to share Jesus.
- Remember to have an attitude of Praise before sharing the Lord.
- Remember to put on the whole armor of God
- Stay away from questions that gender strife. Don't argue about doctrinal issues.
- Stay focused on presenting salvation. Don't get distracted on other issues.
- Don't spend a lot of time with time wasters. There are a lot of people who really are hungry for the word of God. The word of God says, "redeem the time because the days are evil."
- Remember, that the leader takes charge in the conversation and the remainder of the team stands back a few feet. So, as not to crowd the individual being talked to.
- Remember, a soft answer turns away wrath, but harsh words stir up anger.

- When finished praying, ask the individual if they have any other prayer needs.
- Remember to always walk in love and wisdom towards the people you're talking to.
- Don't tell people what's wrong with them. Tell them what God's word says about them.
- Encourage and exhort the people that you pray with.
- Don't get involved in other peoples problems on the streets. If you see something that is serious, call the police at 911.
- Finally, give the glory and honor to God, for it is Him that works in you both to will and to do of His good pleasure.

Things to Remember

- Know that God has given you an Assignment (Mark 16:15-20)
- Know that God has given you His Ability (2 Corinthians 3:5-6)
- Know that God has given you His Authority (Luke 9:1-2), (Luke 10:19)
- Know that God has Anointed you with the Holy Ghost and power (Acts 1:8)
- Know that God wants you to give Him your Availability (Isaiah 6:8)

In Conclusion

If you have finished reading this book and God is tugging at your heart to know Him intimately and be assured that when your life ends someday, you will spend eternity with Him. Then I invite you to say this prayer and mean it with your heart. Then tell someone what you have done. (Romans 10:9-10).

God in Heaven, I know that I'm a sinner and I need your help. I believe in my heart that Jesus Christ is your son, that He died on the cross for my sins and shed His precious blood and You raised Him from the dead. Jesus, right now, I open the door of my heart and invite You to come in. Make Yourself real to me. Take control of my life. Keep me from evil and make me the person You want me to be. Be my Lord and Saviour.

Now that you have asked Jesus into your heart. Be sure to get into God's Word and find a good Bible believing church and get ready to see God work in your life like never before.

Your Brother in Christ,

Pastor Nick Kinn

Pastor Nick Kinn